bravely, bravely
in business

designed and illustrated
by Ric Estrada

bravely, bravely in business

32 ground rules for personal survival and success in your job—any job

Richard R. Conarroe

American Management Association, Inc.

International standard book number: 0-8144-5304-X
Library of Congress catalog card number: 72-78297

Fourth Printing

For Rich and Ron

Gordon Carroll, Nancy Conarroe, Alex Domonkos, Dale Dutton, Fran Fore, Bob Osborn, and Jessie Scippa helped bring this book into being.

Let this then be thine armour
Oh ye brave knight of business
That thy labours
And thine enterprise
Shall be done
With honesty
And with wisdom and honour

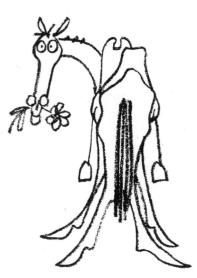

horse sense in business

This is a book on how to be successful in business. What right do I have to write such a book?

I am probably one of the most satisfied guys in business.

I have a stimulating job working with bright, interesting people.

I love what I am doing and I have shaped my job to suit my own work preferences and style.

I have made more money than I would have thought possible a few years ago.

I have a respected position and I enjoy all of the privileges and benefits this brings with it.

I work hard, but my job gives me the time and freedom to do the other things I like to do. Like writing this book.

Because of business I have traveled to many parts of the world.

Through business contacts I have met dozens of beautiful, stimulating girls and I married one of them.

We live in a beautiful waterfront house in Connecticut. We don't have to worry too much about the future. I'm not a millionaire yet but that is mostly because I'm not sure I want to be unless it happens as a by-product of the satisfaction I get from my work.

Just about everything I enjoy in life has come to me from business. I'm looking forward to lots more.

In a word, I'm successful, and I'm still young enough to enjoy it.

Why am I so happy and successful in business? The answer is very simple.

I have a set of horse-sense rules that I try to use as guides in everything I do. I developed these rules one by one, over the years.

I am lucky because my jobs have put me in touch with countless successful businessmen. I have had the chance to question many of them at length about their success.

My horse-sense rules have come partly from what I

have learned by studying others. These rules have been shaped and sharpened, however, by my own trial and error, by my own victories and defeats, by my own successes and failures.

This book has two purposes:

First, to warn you of mistakes most people make in their business careers and help you avoid them.

Second, to give you the makings of a solid code of self-management that you know will hold up in everyday business use.

Whether you are at the beginning, middle, or near the end of your business life, you can profitably adopt these 32 guides. You have my absolute assurance that they will make you more successful than you would otherwise be.

This book is especially for younger men and women in business who do not yet have much experience. I can vividly recall what it is like to be a beginner in business. I remember my feeling of uncertainty and insecurity—of wanting to succeed but not knowing what the rules were. Of not knowing what the determining factors of my success would be. Of not having any frame of reference by which to judge the things that happened to me.

Lacking any training, experience, or guidelines, I had to move slowly and cautiously instead of marching bravely ahead.

I hope this book helps you march bravely ahead.

RICHARD R. CONARROE

1

Pick the people who can most strongly determine your success and stay in direct, personal, continuous touch with them.

Don't believe for a minute you can personally control what happens to you in business.

You can't. Again and again your destiny is wrapped in decisions made by someone else. Your only hope is to influence those decisions.

Every job has its vital contacts—people who can push you forward or back. Sometimes they can make or break you.

Your boss . . . a mentor . . . a key customer . . . a specific subordinate . . . an information source . . . these may be the people who are your vital contacts.

Most of us are smart enough to identify our obvious vital contacts. Sometimes we overlook the less obvious ones. That is a costly mistake.

Equally expensive is to neglect a relationship with a vital contact once it is established. Instead of staying in direct, personal, continuous touch with him, it is tempting to turn your attention to more pressing matters. That is like assuming a fire will keep burning even if you don't throw on another log.

There are two kinds of vital contacts in business.

STATUS QUO CONTACTS help you maintain your position without losing strength or ground.

STATUS EXCELSIOR CONTACTS are those that help you move forward. Examples—

The company president: Status quo contact—the executive vice president. Status excelsior contact—the president of another company he is trying to acquire.

Public relations man: Status quo contact—an important editor. Status excelsior contact—the board chairman's daughter.

The salesman: Status quo contact—a bread and butter customer. Status excelsior contact—the big account he has been working on for a year.

The boss's son: Status quo contact—Dad. Status excelsior contact—Dad.

The bright junior executive: Status quo contact—his

boss. Status excelsior contact—the man he met on the plane who could offer him a much bigger job.

No matter how permanent your vital contacts may seem, don't expect them to last. Only a few do. People you depend on now may not be there for you to depend on tomorrow. They may move on, you may move on, or your relationship with them may change.

Business relationships are more like love affairs than marriage. They flower and fade, and sometimes flower again or die.

One way to measure the quality of a relationship is by how much compromise it requires. Every human relationship requires some compromise, but the best require only a little. Decide what price you are willing to pay to maintain a critical contact. If it becomes too compromising or too costly, find a way to replace it.

The rule calls for *direct, personal, continuous* contact.

DIRECT: that means no intermediaries. There are certain things you can delegate in business and certain things you can't. Staying in touch with your vital contacts is one that you can't. Do it yourself.

PERSONAL: that means handshaking, face-to-face, eyeball-to-eyeball, jawbone-to-jawbone contact whenever possible. Even arm-over-the-shoulder-type contact if that is appropriate. Letters are fine. Telephone calls are great. But face-to-face is better.

CONTINUOUS: That means steady, constant, never-ending, ceaseless. It is the opposite of sporadic, when convenient, erratic, occasional.

Brother, neglecting your vital contacts is like throwing money away. Worse, it is like throwing time away.

Never assume that the way things are today is the way they will be tomorrow—or even after lunch.

Business is like a turning kaleidoscope; the picture keeps changing.

To be caught unprepared by change is silly. You should know that change is always about to happen. Fortunately. Otherwise we would all be bored out of our minds.

The turmoil of business is what keeps you from stagnating, puts the zest in your job, and creates your opportunities.

Everyday—sometimes faster—rules change, priorities change, stock prices change, styles change, weather changes, costs change, trends change, ideas change, tastes change, ways of doing things change, values change, other people change, and you change. All these changes have a direct or indirect effect on your job.

Here's one thing that doesn't change: some people in business cling to the idea that things will stay put. Even people who have been around for a while remain in this category. They live in an unreal world and a lot of them have ulcers.

There are two kinds of change: cyclical and linear.

CYCLICAL CHANGE is mere ebb and flow. What changes today will change back tomorrow.

LINEAR CHANGE is forward motion, from the old to the new, otherwise known as progress. Sometimes linear change makes things better; it almost always makes things more complicated.

There is no shield against change. For example, being in a strategic job doesn't make you safe from cyclical change. Engineers could name their own price in the late sixties and were a drug on the market in the early seventies.

Another thing about change: the higher you go in an organization, the greater the impact of change on your job. At times the president of your company probably feels like a skipper zigzagging through a stormy battle zone while his ship is still under construction. He struggles to get the ship on course and just when he succeeds he has to change course because of a shoal or the diabolical strategy of the enemy.

Take your pick. You can find jobs where change is slow and unspectacular. Or you can find jobs where every mail delivery or telephone call represents a potential adventure. But you cannot find a job where things stay the same.

Like many forces in business, change may confound your career if you don't learn to use it to advantage.

For most changes there are plenty of advance signals. Learn to read the signals and you can usually predict when and how change is going to happen—or even postpone or prevent it.

Most of the change that will affect you begins in someone's mind: a customer's, the boss's, a fellow employee's. People transmit their as-yet-unspoken thoughts in many ways: facial expressions and body language, unrelated complaints or compliments, casual daydreams, moods and manners.

Sometimes a person's total lack of communication tells you everything you need to know about his intentions.

Once you learn to read the forecasts, analyze the directional flow of change. Which way are things going? Practice spotting trends and patterns in the formative stage, especially those that will change your job. Learn to distinguish real trends from mere fizzlers. When you see change coming, adjust your course to compensate for it or take advantage of it.

There is an even better way to use change: be the person who creates it. Instead of responding to change started by somebody else, start it yourself. That way you know what is going to happen and you build a reputation as a trend-setter.

The phrase "business as usual" contradicts itself. Business is never as usual.

**No matter what your job is,
think of yourself as a salesman.**

If you are in business, you are a salesman.

It is not a matter of your choice.

You may be called junior executive, engineer, plant manager, secretary, carpenter, chemist, designer, vice president—it doesn't matter. You are still a salesman.

All day every day you are selling people on your
ideas, selling them on your company, and, most important, selling them on yourself.

You may be doing it skillfully or poorly, thoughtfully
or unknowingly, successfully or unsuccessfully. But you
are still selling. All the time.

You may say you have no talent as a salesman. That
is not the point. Most of the people who are called salesmen have little or no natural talent for selling either. Many
of them succeed anyway.

The kind of salesmanship we are talking about here
is more a matter of attitude than talent.

If you can create in your mind, then refine and
maintain, the right kind of sales consciousness, you will
increase the degree of success in everything you do. It
will reflect in the quality of your work, your attitude
toward your job and toward the people you work with. It
will even influence the clarity and content of your ideas.

If you display the enthusiasm of a good salesman,
you soon find that at least some of that enthusiasm becomes real. It will show up in the product you build, the
service you perform, the report you write, the telephone
calls you make, the letters you dictate, and in what you
say to the job candidate you interview or your boss when
he takes you to lunch.

Many of the ways you sell yourself are indirect. You
don't have to be up on a soapbox beating a drum for yourself. Wherever you are, whatever you are doing, just
standing or sitting there, if others can see you, you are
merchandise on display. You can merchandise yourself
well or poorly by displaying your most favorable or least
favorable characteristics.

There is a reason why first impressions are so lasting. When someone first comes into contact with you, he gets a flash flood of instantaneous information about you. He may not consciously catalog all the impressions you give him, but he is getting them and storing them away.

He notices your bearing, hears whether your voice reflects confidence, feels the strength of your handshake.

You signal still more information to him by the way you have packaged yourself. On the basis of your dress and grooming, he decides whether you are a formal or an informal person, relaxed or turned on, careful or careless, conservative or perhaps a pacesetter.

It is amazing how much information a person's desk, workplace, or office communicates about him. By simply walking into a man's office, even when he isn't there, you can often discover a world of information about him. Is it designed as a workplace, or a showplace, or both? Is it tastefully and individually decorated to reflect the individuality of the man himself? Or is it the kind of slick, expensive-looking office that reflects the taste of his decorator?

The appearance of an office can tell you whether it is occupied by a busy man who is in full control of his job, or by a mere paper-shuffler . . . by a man who enjoys his work, or hates it . . . an iconoclast or conformist . . . a man who has his own ideas or is more comfortable with someone else's.

What is true of a man's office is equally true of his car. It tells you what he thinks of himself. Have you ever met someone for lunch, opened the door of his car, and found the floor covered with cigarette butts, crumpled maps, children's toys, and crushed containers from a drive-in restaurant? Tells you something about your friend, doesn't it?

You may work in a broom closet and be unable to afford anything better than a five-year-old Volkswagen, but you can still use these things as indirect personal sales aids. The same goes for your home, your other possessions, and your personal habits. Not to mention your wife and kids.

Business is made up of buyers and sellers. A good rule of thumb to keep in mind is that sellers earn more than buyers.

In any buyer-seller relationship, the seller is the one who takes charge. He is the aggressor, the one who controls the situation. If he is successful, the seller succeeds in getting the buyer to see things his way, bend to his will, and take the action he wants taken.

One key point: people love to be sold. They love to see a good salesman in action. They love to buy from a salesman who has truly sold them.

Most people expect a salesman to sell—hard. They are disappointed if he doesn't. They want to be sold after they buy as well as before. When a salesman turns off his salesmanship after the sale is made, the buyer is not just disappointed—he feels cheated.

If you are in business to have your ego massaged, to be courted and entertained, to be appealed to—in a word, to be sold to—then get into a job that puts you into the role of a buyer. If you do it right, it can be a fairly rewarding job.

But if you are in business to be creative and to be highly rewarded for the value you create, get into a job that puts you into the role of a salesman.

Buyers like to think that they are in the driver's seat. Let them. Every good salesman knows that the seller is really in the driver's seat.

This doesn't mean that when you are in the buyer's role you must be passive. You can become the seller in any relationship, any situation, even when you are supposedly being sold. The salesman is always the aggressor, always on the offensive, never in a passive or defensive role.

So be a salesman. Or at least think of yourself as one.

Never fail to consider the future significance of what you say and do.

It is a classic plot line. You find it in every kind of literature, from the Old Testament and Shakespeare to Charles Atlas ads and fairy tales.

There is this little runty guy that the big boys laugh at and pick on. By some amazing feat or circumstance,

depending on the kind of story it is, this weakling is trans-
formed into a veritable powerhouse and gets to an exalted
position. He naturally opts to give his favors to those who
treated him considerately back when. Meanwhile he
watches with interest and perhaps amusement as the
bullies who kicked sand in his face now gnash their teeth
and tear their hair for not having been more farsighted.

It is a plot line that persists not only in literature but
in business. The reason is simple: most people in business
are decidedly shortsighted. Faced with the urgency of
dealing with a conglomeration of immediate problems,
they fail to consider that each word and action is another
brush stroke in the record they are painting of their
business life.

There is a double reason for making friends in
business. First, it makes working more pleasant. Second,
some of the friends you make now will cross your path in
new capacities later. Unimportant people have an un-
canny, almost diabolical way of turning up in pivotal
positions.

Remember that acne-faced file clerk you failed to
pay any attention to in your last job? She could be the
boss's secretary in your next job.

Remember that salesman you brusquely brushed off
because you were too busy to be courteous to him? He
could turn up working for your key customer next month.

Remember the supplier who thinks you canceled his
order unfairly? He could turn up as a member of the City
Council, heading a committee to investigate your industry.

Remember the guy from your plant with the stalled
car who tried to flag you down while you were racing to
an important meeting? He may remind you of that day a

couple of years from now when he faces you across the bargaining table.

Big people in business are used to being paid attention to; they expect it. Little people—small cogs doing routine work—are not used to it and so appreciate it all the more when you notice them as individuals. Secretaries . . . lab assistants . . . telephone operators . . . receptionists . . . junior assistants . . . elevator operators . . . handymen . . . bookkeepers and file clerks . . . all the so-called little people in business—make friends with them, pay attention to them, listen to them, remember their names. Don't do it *just* because they may be able to help you someday, but *also* because they may be able to help you someday.

This does not mean to avoid taking all actions that will offend someone. You can't survive that way. To be successful you must exert yourself, express yourself, be critical when criticism is called for, make decisions, and take aggressive actions that serve the interests of the company as a whole rather than the interests of isolated individuals.

When you do these things, some people are going to be hurt and offended. However, there is a way to keep the resentment and hurt feelings to a minimum. It is simply to take the trouble to explain to the affected people what you are doing and why.

Most reasonable people, even when they are personally getting hurt, will accept your actions without a grudge if you have sound reasons for what you are doing and explain these reasons in terms they can understand.

For example, one of the most distasteful jobs in business is firing someone. Yet if you handle it properly, most of the bitterness can usually be removed from even this negative experience. If you have valid reasons for firing someone, and if you present these reasons to him in clear, unquestionable terms, he will usually accept his fate gallantly. In fact, it is surprising how many people accept being fired with a sense of relief instead of resentment. Most people who are in the wrong job know it. If you can fire such a person without damaging his ego, and with counsel on how he should redirect his talents, you may make a friend instead of an enemy. Later, when he turns up in your business life again, he may even thank you for the surgery you performed on his career.

Like a picture you might paint, your own business record is a form of creative expression. It speaks for you. If the record you are making is unplanned and thoughtlessly composed, it will probably turn out as a confused jumble, a canvas you would rather hide than display. You may be able to convince some people that it is a free-form style of interpretive modern art, but anyone with real appreciation and knowledge will see through that sham.

The true business artist develops a plan for his painting. He may not know at the outset how he is going to execute the plan. He may alter the plan from time to time. He may not know how the final painting will turn out. Nevertheless each line, shape, and color he adds will serve to increase the meaning and the beauty of his theme.

Consistency is essential if you want to achieve more than transient success. What good is it if your words and actions create a splash of success today but lead to mediocrity or failure tomorrow?

Sometimes the short-term and long-term values of

something you do are consistent, but sometimes they are conflicting. For example, suppose you are offered a well-paying job that will give you the kind of experience you want but where the company itself has a bad reputation. Consider whether the long-range cost of including that company on your record outweighs the immediate advantages of the job.

It should be effortlessly easy to measure the future significance of what you are doing today. If you find it difficult, it means your long-range goals are not specific enough.

It is impossible to measure anything without some kind of yardstick or standard of comparison. Your goals provide this necessary yardstick. The clearer and more specific your goals, the easier it is to judge whether today's decisions and actions will contribute to or detract from your success in the future.

Like everything else in your career, your goals will change, of course. You are probably evolving and refining your goals all the time. The change may be steady and rapid, but, like the changes in a growing child seen every day, it goes unnoticed. Thus it is wise to take inventory of your long-range goals at regular intervals—certainly every year and preferably every six months or three months.

If your goals have changed, even slightly, review your present activities; make adjustments in what you are doing now to match what you want to happen later.

How easy it is to be opportunistic in business. And, in the long run, how costly.

In business as in other indoor sports, position isn't everything—but almost.

To put it bluntly, position equals power. It often takes the place of ability.

A position is good or bad in relation to others that are worse or better. If you are in the wrong position and someone else is in the right position—tough luck, Charlie. He uses you—or misuses you.

Your position is determined by a combination of things.

Your *level* in the organization is one.

Size is another. You can become a chief executive by incorporating your family and appointing yourself president. But your position is meaningless.

What you do is another. In some companies the financial VP outranks the sales VP who outranks the manufacturing VP. Generally the broader your function the better.

Reputation is another. To be recognized as the best in the business gives you a dominant position.

Less competent people get many of the strategic positions in business. Once there they have the power to perpetuate themselves.

This causes the management pontificators to worry about the shortage of good managers. But there is no such shortage. A company can prosper nicely with a ratio of about one competent manager for every five incompetent. In some companies, still successful, this ratio extends to one-to-ten or more.*

Picture a company miraculously staffed by competent managers only. This company would explode in growth because of its lack of incompetents. Vast numbers of additional managers would then be required. Most of them would be incompetent. This would bring the ratio back into balance and start the pontificators worrying all over again.

It is easier to deal with competent people in strategic

---

* Incompetent may be too strong a word. Translate it here to mean less than adequately qualified. All incompetent executives are not *totally* incompetent. Most have enough competence to disguise their incompetence. That's the trouble. Their incompetence may not show up until the chips are down.

positions than incompetents, particularly those directly above you.

The one thing incompetent people fear most is the competence of the people under them.

When you are better qualified than your boss, the natural tendency is to be resentful and to make sure other people know it. This is self-defeating.

The secret is to make your boss look good even though it hurts.

Example. You go to your boss with a great idea; he takes it to his boss as his idea. (A lot of teeth have been gnashed over just this situation.)

CHOICE ONE: You express your resentment. This puts you *and* your boss on the defensive and makes both of you look bad. Men at higher levels wonder whether they want you working for them.

CHOICE TWO: You swallow hard and let your boss have the credit. You compliment him for the extra touches he added and the way he sold the idea to the brass.

Choice two wins. When you first activate this policy, you feel like a cross between a hypocrite and a martyr. With practice it gets easier. And it pays off.

Why? Because your action tells your boss you are not a threat to him. In gratitude, he will start tooting your horn, which is six times better than tooting it yourself.

Sure, he will take credit for your ability. He will say he trained and developed you. What do you care? Nothing suits a talented man's interests better than to have a lot of people claiming credit for his talent.

You can move up in position by getting people to push you up and pull you up. You can do that by making them *want* you to succeed. And you can do that by making them look good.

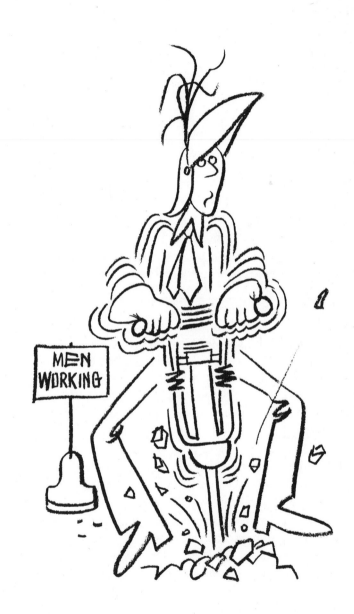

**Know what it is you can do better
than anyone else—and do that.**

Most people in business do not properly use their real talents. Instead of building on what they do best, they go off in other directions. This is why most people in business experience only a fraction of the success they could enjoy. The same goes for companies.

Highly successful people are generally no smarter or more skilled than the others. Their secret is that they know how to make full use of their limited brains and talents while they are building experience.

Almost every individual (and company) is great at some things, mediocre at a lot of other things, and a clod at some other things.

The minute you get away from the things you do best, you are abandoning your all-important competitive advantage. Even the weakness you overcome may give you only amateur standing.

Specialize in the areas where you are great and you will be richer, happier, and more secure.

The sad part is that many people (and companies) never even realize what their true talents are.

One reason is that you can easily be misled by initial success. You may have experienced success because of *one* thing you did well. It is tempting to assume that your success is evidence that you did *everything* well. Right there you violate logic and start to defeat yourself.

Take an example. You have experienced great success selling weathervanes to farmers. You conclude that you are therefore a great salesman. You take a bigger job selling machine tools to industrial plants—and fall on your face.

Why? Figure it out. Maybe it is because you are great at selling to *farmers*. If so, then maybe your success lies in selling tractors and other high-commission farm machinery, rather than in trying to prove you are the greatest machine tool salesman in the world.

Don't misunderstand. To specialize does not mean to stagnate. As you continue to accumulate experience, broaden your scope. But do it from a position of strength, not weakness, by building on your best skills.

The weathervane salesman will need to expand his scope tremendously before he gets to be a successful farm equipment dealer. He will need to learn finance, market research, mechanics, farming, politics, accounting, and a dozen other things. As he expands his horizons, he may discover that he is great in some of these areas and only mediocre in others. His success will then depend on his ability to get the help of other people who are great in the areas where he is not.

What is true for a salesman with manure on his boots is equally true for a man in a business suit working in a big organization.

FIRST, know what your true talents and limitations are. This takes soul-searching, an honest appraisal of yourself, some trial and error.

SECOND, build a personal growth plan that is based squarely on what you can do best. Get into a job that you can do better than anyone else. Don't keep changing specialties; every time you do you lose ground.

THIRD, keep learning, keep expanding your scope, keep building experience.

FOURTH, develop the one indispensable skill you must have to succeed in business—the ability to pick great people. As your responsibilities increase, particularly your management responsibilities, lean on the people who are great where you are weak.

FIFTH, never forget your limitations. You will find there is more than enough success to be had in the areas where you excel; it simply isn't necessary to reach for success in areas where you don't. The temptation is to

grow by venturing into new areas. Up to a point this is
healthy and pays off. But as you get further away from
the basics you know best, the ice gets thinner.

You hear a lot of talk about the difference between
generalists and specialists in business. Much of what you
hear is bunk. Especially misleading is the notion that
specialists don't make good managers. This makes it
sound as if the way to be a manager is not to be good at
anything.

Successful business requires a combination of general-
ized thinking and specialized know-how. But we are all
specialists. Don't ever forget it. A generalist is just a special kind of specialist. He has learned to spread his special
skills over a broader area. He has learned to manage, and
that is quite a specialty in itself.

These special specialists called generalists are the
ones who get to be the top men in the top corporations.
If you have—or think you can develop—the combination
of unique skills required to handle one of those jobs, then
set your sights on top management.

Don't feel guilty, however, if your self-analysis indicates you don't want it or you can't make it. You can be
just as rich and happy as a specialist in your own field,
doing what you do better than anyone else. If you don't
think so, ask any successful advertising copywriter, or
the successful owner of a chain of specialty shops, or a
successful franchised food operator, or a successful management consultant, or a successful lawyer, designer, or
architect—or a successful anybody, for that matter. Part
of your compensation will come in the form of enjoying
what you are doing.

Some years ago a new season of TV shows was

being planned for Perry Como. The producer had worked out ideas for skits, dance routines, guest stars, jokes. He asked Perry Como if he thought the format would work.

He replied in his usual relaxed manner, "Well, if it doesn't work, I can always sing."

Perry Como obviously understood something about success in business.

Never say anything about anyone you wouldn't say in exactly the same way to his face.

Sarcasm, innuendo, and ridicule are the tools of the business hack.

Go ahead, drop a subtly unflattering remark about a rival to your boss. See what happens. You will probably succeed in undermining the boss's confidence in the man. But look what you do to yourself. Your boss has got to wonder—consciously or subconsciously—whether you are using the same technique to undermine him.

Mediocre people who have topped out in business spend a lot of their time trying to bring others down to their own level of mediocrity. Don't join them. You don't have to condemn them; just don't join them.

You can learn a great deal about a company by listening to the way the people talk about each other, about customers, and suppliers. Their comments reflect mutual respect or lack of it, the kind of spirit that exists in the company, how much teamwork there is, how busy people are, and whether there is the right amount of management control. If people have the time and inclination to gossip about each other, it is a signal that they are not busy enough.

The watercooler, long favored by cartoonists, has lost its place as the chief meeting place for office gossip. The telephone has taken over because of several advantages. Everyone has one right on his or her desk. It is reasonably private. It gives people the appearance of working. Walk through some seemingly busy offices and, at any given time, half or more of the people will be talking on the telephone. Tune in and you find that fewer than half of these are talking business. Many are talking about each other.

In some offices there is enough backbiting going on to satisfy an old maid's sewing circle. All a person has to do is leave the room to become the topic of discussion.

Business backbiting may be fun—it must be, there is so much of it—but it is a costly luxury. It is time-consuming, distracting, wastes mental energy, and it's a sure sign of weakness and insecurity in the person who is doing the talking.

A strong manager is frequently an easy target for ridicule. Little people like to take out their resentments against a big man. It is not uncommon to see a boss or business owner given great deference in his presence, then ridiculed as a clown in his absence for his personal idiosyncrasies. Such a man seldom fails to realize what is being said behind his back. He puts up with it because he needs his subordinates almost as much as they need him.

One very simple way to win the recognition of a powerful man of this kind is to give him the honesty and respect he deserves, in his presence and out of it.

To succeed in business you need all the help you can get. You get support by building people up, not tearing them down. When you have something critical or negative to say about someone, have the guts to say it to him directly, or in his presence. That way you avoid even giving the impression of subterfuge.

If you are successful you can count on being talked about behind your back. Don't reciprocate. Backbiting is the cheapest game in business.

Search for the seeds of victory in every disaster—and the seeds of disaster in every victory.

Some people in business are lucky. They get fired, lose a crucial customer, launch an idea that flops, lose out to a rival, or experience some other gut-wrenching setback just when it will do them the most good.

If you think this sounds like some kind of masochistic nut talking, then you haven't experienced enough disasters in your career. You haven't learned that you can make your greatest progress without knowing it at the least likely times.

The best time and place to make a fresh start is when you are flat on your pazzutz. For one thing, you are free of all the encumbrances that probably helped cause your disaster in the first place. You don't have to maintain your dignity because when you are flat on your pazzutz you haven't got any. Nobody can expect you to adhere to any kind of established performance pattern because the pattern has been broken.

In many respects, flat on your pazzutz is a wonderful place to be.

The trouble is, when you are down there it is hard to view your situation from a positive perspective. But if you want to make your recovery rapid and dramatic, force this point of view into your mind. You will amaze yourself by the energy, ideas, and motivation it gives you.

To build this frame of mind, start with the idea that a necessary ingredient of success is change. If things don't change for you, how will you reach your success? Continuous improvement is what leads to success, and things can't improve unless they change.

And brother, if there is one thing that creates change it is defeat. It very thoroughly gets you out of your rut. It changes your direction (usually from forward to back). It gets your mind on the subject of survival. It destroys habit patterns—which obviously weren't working. It makes you question your priorities, your goals, your attitudes, your methods, why you are in business in the first place.

A defeat shows that something was wrong; otherwise you wouldn't have been defeated. At the very least it shows you failed to protect yourself against a contingency. Okay, if something was wrong, now is the ideal time to make changes. If you can survive a major defeat and come back, you are sure to be stronger in many ways. You can usually find the makings of an even bigger victory in the rubble of defeat—provided you are a winner, that is.

If it is a serious defeat you have suffered and you have lost a lot, look at it this way: you have that much less to carry as you start back up the side of the mountain.

Now consider the other side of the picture.

Just as you can make your greatest advances after a setback, you are most susceptible to defeat right after a major victory. When everything is going great and you seem to be making real progress, watch out! If you let your defenses down, you may get hit by a falling brick.

Victors tend to get careless. How many times have you seen a man defeated by his own success? It can happen in any number of ways, but basically it happens when a man takes too much comfort in his success, drops his guard, relaxes his vigilance, and leaves himself vulnerable. Business doesn't often forgive a man for relaxing his vigilance.

The same applies to companies. You or your company may be most vulnerable when you are most successful—and you may face your greatest opportunity when disaster has struck.

There are three things to do to turn disaster into success:

First, be ready for it before it happens. Have a contingency plan. Ask yourself a lot of "What if . . ." questions. What if I lose my job? What if Rogers gets to be branch manager instead of me? What if we don't make a profit this year? What if the union strikes, or the economy turns sour, or a competitor beats us out with a new product?

Second, analyze why it happened. You must have been doing something wrong—or doing it at the wrong time, or at the wrong place, or with the wrong people, or in the wrong way, or for the wrong reasons. This time, as you try again, make sure you have whatever was missing the first time, or get rid of what you should not have had.

Third, counterattack. When a man is down, his frame of mind tends to be defensive rather than offensive. This is natural, but it adds self-defeat to the defeat he already has enough of. By taking the offensive with a counterattack as soon as you have suffered a defeat, you not only force yourself to start thinking positively again; sometimes you can turn disaster into immediate victory. The reason counterattacks work is that defeated people are supposed to act defeated, and victors are so busy being victors in their overextended positions that they are surprised when supposedly beaten people start moving forward.

The next time disaster strikes, fight off the urge to put your tail between your legs. Ignore the disgrace of it all and look for a new way to put the pieces back together. Maybe the new combination will get you farther than you could have gone otherwise.

There are also three things to do about the dangers of victory.

First, use your success to further strengthen your position. Take your cue from the most successful men in business. They never stop competing. They stay right out there on the cutting edge.

Second, think negative thoughts. What if . . .

Third, start moving toward a further goal. The biggest reward in business is the pleasure you get from *going* somewhere, not from *being* somewhere.

**Don't lie. If you can't tell
the truth, keep quiet. When you
start lying, you are dead.**

Figure 1 shows a breakdown of liars, fabricators, and truth tellers in business.

One of the smartest moves you can make is to get into the third category and stay there.

You will make life a whole lot simpler for everyone.

Figure 1.

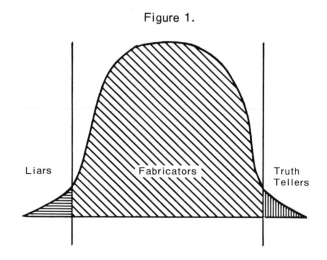

There are so few people in business who always tell the truth that just being one of them makes you special. It takes guts to tell the truth every time. And it takes time to build a reputation as someone who does tell the truth every time. To get that reputation you have to prove yourself—often repeatedly—under fire. But it sure is worth it.

Most business people are fabricators, otherwise known as bull-throwers. Your everyday fabricator serves up the truth with a portion of bull stirred in. How much bull depends. You have to separate the truth by sizing up the situation and the man.

There are all kinds of fabricators. One type tells you only what you want to hear. Among others are lily-gilders, wishful thinkers, moon promisers, smokescreen specialists, and public relations men.

There are few out-and-out liars in business. This is

not due to a short supply. It is due to a fantastically high mortality rate. Liars can't survive. Those who linger on are mostly in the lower ranks.

Figure 2 shows how few liars there are in management. Survival of the fittest is the law, and liars are not fit to manage anybody.

What few liars there are raise havoc. It is hard to spot them early. Once you do spot them, the best strategy is simply to stay away from them. They are the people who not only give business a bad name, but they can give you a bad name if you let them become too closely identified with you.

Figure 2. Prevalence of liars in management.

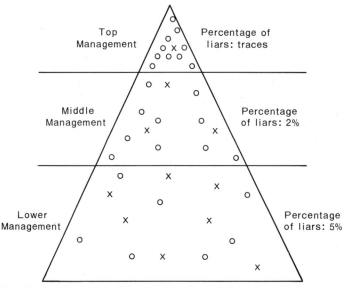

The X's are liars. The O's are men who consistently tell the truth. The rest of the management triangle is filled with fabricators.

One sad thing about liars is that most (but not all) liars lie to themselves as much as they lie to others. A few own up to being liars, but most go through their whole lives never realizing they are suffering from this terrible disease.

As with fabricators, there are several species of liars in business: pathological liars, habitual liars, only-under-pressure liars, little white liars, and conspiratorial liars, to name just a few. Each group has its own special way of justifying, explaining away, or even glorifying its lies.

One common false notion is that anyone in business must be dishonest and untruthful. The fact is that businessmen are comparatively the most truthful people around. Not necessarily by choice; they have to be. Today businessmen are watched, prodded, reviewed, studied, poked, examined, questioned, challenged, inspected, policed, criticized, quizzed, threatened, controlled, patrolled, computerized, bargained with, blamed, restricted, dictated to, demanded of, regulated, researched, red-flagged, and cross-examined by more public and private agencies, bureaus, committees, unions, journalists, stock-holders, consumers, politicians, muckrakers, defenders of the faith, pressure groups, social commentators, mothers, and competitors than anybody else, and certainly more than they can possibly satisfy.

It is easy to define a liar. He is someone who has no respect for the truth and regularly departs from it. He tells the truth only by haphazard coincidence or because the truth seems to serve him better than a lie.

It is also easy to define a fabricator. He is someone who respects the truth but permits himself the conven-

ience of operating in the wide swath of gray area that
exists between truth and lie. A fabricator stretches the
truth. He bends it a little. Or a lot.

There are many words to describe liars and fabricators. Significantly, there is no word for someone who
always tells the truth.

That shows how rare a bird he is.

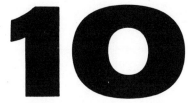

Never expect someone to keep a secret. There are no secrets.

Here is an experiment to prove that no secret is sacred in your organization. Give an innocent tidbit of confidential information to someone at a remote branch of the grapevine. Then see how long it takes to get back to you.

The experiment will test your antennae. Most secrets travel at supersonic speed. If your secret does not come back quickly, you may be tuned to the wrong frequency. You are in serious trouble when others know what is going on and you don't.

There are four ways to use the knowledge that people don't keep secrets.

First, don't have secrets. Avoid subterfuge of all kinds. Ask yourself why a secret seems necessary. Is it to hide facts you are ashamed of? Then change the facts. Is it to keep someone in the dark about something he has a right to know? Then the secret is the same as a lie.

Second, if you must have a secret, minimize the risk. The only pure secret is the one you keep yourself. Each person you tell multiplies the probability of a leak. Tell the fewest number of people possible. Five is probably the maximum. Beyond that, the barn door is wide open.

Pick your confidants carefully. It even pays to test them. Use an unimportant secret to test for leaks.

Once you have shared a secret with someone (even your secretary who has secret built right into her name) operate on the theory that it will be violated. Sooner or later every secret leaks—usually sooner.

If your secret leaks and you don't know it, you become the one who is in the dark.

Third, use "secrets" as a subtle way to communicate. Suppose you are a junior executive and you want to make known to your boss—without telling him—that you have started a night school course to improve yourself. Just pick a secretary who is pals with the boss's secretary. Tell her you are taking the course but you don't want the boss to know about it until you are finished.

That night, in class, you can take comfort in the boss's knowledge of your ambitiousness.

Fourth, use "secrets" to gather information. Those office gossips make good CIA agents. Keep in touch with one or more.

Remember that you have to buy information with information. An effective intelligence agent must trade fact for fact, news for news, rumor for rumor.

Therefore, never underestimate the power of information you possess. Since it won't be a secret long anyway, you might as well use it while it still has salable value. Get rid of it while you can, before it rots, or explodes. Every secret carries the seeds of its own destruction. And if you are not careful—yours.

Bet on people—but be prepared to lose.

Most of the people you bet on in business will be losers. But that is no reason to quit betting. If you don't bet you automatically lose. If you do bet, a few of the people you bet on will be winners. Those few will more than make up for the many losers.

One of the few things the human race has going for it is its ability to organize for group effort. Self-interest dictates teamwork. In business you can't make it alone; the competition is too stiff. To be limited by your own personal resources is pretty limiting, no matter how good you are.

In order to survive and succeed, you must join or lead other people.

Synergism is a word commonly used in connection with mergers. When you put the right two companies together, the united company is worth more than the sum of the two companies separately, and that's synergism. "Two plus two equals five" is the way businessmen like to say this.

Until the happy day when you are leading your company and negotiating mergers, keep the concept of synergism in mind. You can use it then but you can also use it now.

Why? Because it applies to people as well as companies. You can apply the dynamics of synergism by putting the right people together. You plus Joe may equal four, but you plus Sam may equal five.

When you bet on people you put your destiny in their hands. Here are a few of the things you can expect:

Deception
Treachery
"Let George do it" (assuming your name is George)
Incompetence
Overpowering self-interest
Egotism
Laziness

Personality conflicts
Pomposity
Temperament

Until you learn to expect these things, they will give you
many nights of agonized tossing and turning. It is the
price you have to pay. Nobody said you had to go into
business. But if you are going to be in the game you have
to play it. If you are going to play it, you are going to
lose as well as win. How much you win or lose depends
on the people you pick to work with, or to work with you.

Everything in business is a gamble, but the biggest
gamble you make is on people.

**Unsolvable problems don't disrupt
the routine; they are the routine.**

Each person in business has in the recesses of his
mind a serene picture of the way things ought to be.
Orderly. Organized. Consistent. Cooperative. Smooth-
running.

Part of everyone's job is to try to make things match

this image. No one ever succeeds. As a result, some people get frustrated and wind up with ulcers. The mark of a successful man is that he takes his failure philosophically. He keeps on battling his unsolvable problems, but he doesn't make himself sick over the situation.

Your problem is to distinguish between solvable problems and unsolvable problems. You can defeat yourself either way—by considering an unsolvable problem solvable, or by considering a solvable problem unsolvable.

Solvable problems are like baseballs pitched while you are up at bat. The balls keep coming. If you take a swat, you may miss completely, hit poorly (which may be just as bad), or hit well.

The difference between baseball and business is that in business if your batting average is good enough, you can stay at bat indefinitely. Everyone who has ever played baseball knows that being the batter is the real fun of the game. Everyone experienced in business knows that the real fun of that game is being in a position to make decisions and solve problems.

If a solvable problem is like a baseball, then trying to solve an unsolvable problem is like trying to pick up a blob of mercury with your fingers. All you accomplish —temporarily—is to change its shape, cause it to move, or split it into pieces.

One whole category of unsolvable problems is caused by simple supply and demand. Business always provided you with too much of the wrong things and too little of the right things.

For example, one unsolvable problem is that you can never get enough good people; the more you get, the higher your standards become. Your budget is never big enough; the bigger it is, the more ambitious your plans become. For the rest of your business life, you can count on suffering consistently from too little time, too few customers, too little information, not enough materials. At the same time, you will be loaded down with too many costs, too many conflicting ideas, too many mechanical breakdowns, too many broken promises, too many customer complaints, too many union or employee demands when profits are high, and too many angry stockholders when profits are low.

You have no choice except to fight these problems, but you will never solve them.

Another whole category of unsolvable problems stems from competition. Don't make the mistake of thinking of competition as a marketing word. Marketing competition is only the obvious kind. Sure, there are competitors for your markets (other companies). But you and your company also have stiff competition for your profits (governments, unions, landlords). And you have competitors for your position (rivals inside or outside your company). There are competitors for your people (other companies that would like to pirate the good ones). And there are certainly competitors for your most valuable commodity: time.

The dynamics of unsolvable problems creates a balance; your unsolvable problems tend to stay in balance with your ability to cope with them. As your strength increases, your unsolvable problems get bigger. As your unsolvable problems get bigger, they cause your strength to increase. This is the natural process of growth and success in business.

The order of business is disorder. Don't knock your unsolvable problems; without them you would have nothing to succeed at.

**Make as few mistakes as possible.
Assume that any random error
could be fatal.**

    Next time some dimwit advises you to "Learn from your mistakes," punch him in the nose.

    Mistakes are the most costly, destructive way to learn any lesson. If your mistakes are big enough, you may become a real smart individual, but you may not be around to show it.

63

Don't learn from your mistakes. The only thing mistakes teach you is what won't work. Learn from your victories.

Every year thousands of people in business go down the drain because of their thoughtless goofs. Sometimes they take their companies along with them. Over the years, some of the biggest and best-known companies have vanished from the scene because of a single blunder.

How many times have you seen a football team fight its way to the two-yard line in the closing seconds and then lose the game because some klutz fumbled the ball?

Making mistakes in business is like getting lost in your car. After you are lost it takes ten times longer to find your way back than it would have taken to double-check your route in the first place.

In business as in driving, there are all kinds of maps, landmarks, signs, and other guides to keep you from making mistakes. Yet in business as in driving, people continue to barrel ahead, missing turns, and then spending the rest of the day trying to correct their errors and make up for lost time.

Many people in business spend most of their time dealing with their mistakes. Some spend almost all their time at it.

Take a typical sales manager. He has a hundred salesmen. Probably ninety-seven of these salesmen will be fairly competent. The remaining three are the ones who cause most of the sales manager's problems. They are the ones who miss their plane to the sales meeting, cause the majority of customer complaints, promise more than the plant can deliver, botch up important accounts, et cetera.

The sales manager may spend 90 percent of his time trying to correct the mistakes made by 3 percent of his sales force—because he made a mistake in hiring these losers in the first place.

Theoretically, if he had not hired them, he could handle his job in 10 percent of his time. Wouldn't it be great if it worked out that way in practice.

Unfortunately, you can't avoid all mistakes in business because you can't avoid taking risks. You can probably survive in business without taking chances, but you can't succeed. And you certainly can't have any fun.

It is risk-taking ability, says one experienced management consultant, that separates the men from the boys in business—and makes some men worth so much more money than others.

For example, he says, the president of a coal mining company doesn't have to make very many risky decisions. The entire operation of getting coal out of the ground and onto railroad cars is pretty predictable.

The head of a film studio, on the other hand, is called on to make dozens of decisions in connection with each film his company produces. He has to buy the right story, assign the right scriptwriter, pick the right director, sign up the right star—and so on. Any one of these expensive and risky decisions, if wrong, could be fatal.

That's why presidents of film companies get paid so much more than presidents of coal companies. And why they get more of a kick out of their jobs.

Risk taking is like a tightrope. On one side is disaster if you are overconfident; on the other, stagnation if you always play it safe. Neither side is a very desirable place to be. When you fall off the tightrope, it takes time to get back up there, make ready, and start over again. That's why the skilled businessman or businesswoman takes only calculated risks—moving forward at his or her best possible speed, but avoiding missteps that could mean a fall.

One of the most common mistakes business people make is not knowing when to say no.

Take a typical example—one that almost any company could give you its version of.

A small East Coast company has a guy in it who has hatched an ambitious plan to open a West Coast office—with himself as manager, naturally.

Maybe this fellow just wants to move to California for family reasons, but he has this shiny new plan for the company's growth, and he presents it to the president with great enthusiasm and optimism.

The president is hesitant. He knows the company has its hands full with present operations. But here is this eager young fellow champing at the bit to turn the company into a national institution. The president's instincts and better judgment tell him to hold back, but he doesn't want to be chicken. After all, wasn't this great country of ours built by the adventurous, pioneering spirit? Where would we be now without those Conestoga wagons, et cetera?

So the company goes ahead and opens a West Coast office; and because the idea was a mistake, it fails.

The failure itself is costly enough—all that energy siphoned off from the company's base operation where it could have done some good.

Even worse, the president will now spend a large amount of his time during the next six months or year cleaning up the mess. The time, trouble, thinking, distraction, buck-passing, annoyance, conflicts, frustration, injured reputations, lawsuits, and money could have been saved if the president had had the guts to say no when he knew he should have.

The president probably learned something from the experience, but the cost to himself and his company was doubtless a lot more than appears on the surface.

You don't have to be a reactionary to avoid making mistakes; all it usually takes is a little patience.

Plus a realization that business is not as forgiving as the hearts-and-flowers types would like you to believe.

14

**Never fail to consider the pervasive
power of personal self-interest.**

Business exists for one reason: because it satisfies
the healthy and sometimes unhealthy hungers of the
people in it.

Sugarcoat the fact and you are kidding yourself.

You hear all kinds of pap about the role of business.

Its purpose is to provide jobs. Its purpose is to serve society. Its purpose is to satisfy the needs and wants of its customers.

Bull. Business does not run on altruism. It is driven by the self-interest and avarice of the people who put in their time and money.

If you think this sounds like Karl Marx summing up the evils of capitalism, you miss the point.

Every kind of group has something that holds it together. Family members perform their roles out of love for each other. Social clubs stick together for fun. Religions get people to sublimate self-interest for rewards in the next world.

The glue that holds business together is unalloyed personal self-interest. Nobody is in business strictly for love or sport. Business could not survive on promises of glory in the hereafter; the rewards have to be here and now.

The world of business is often called a jungle; the description is apt. Business is a sophisticated, mechanized translation of a natural ecology.

A healthy jungle is a good place for its natural inhabitants to be. Each species survives through constant competitive struggle. The jungle itself stays healthy through the balanced interdependence of all forms of life, each competing for the resources needed to proliferate and expand.

In the business jungle, the same natural laws apply, including survival of the fittest.

You and I work in the business world because we want to, not because we have to. We could find plenty of other interesting and enjoyable ways to use our time and make a living. We are in business because of the big rewards it gives us or promises us. It is the easiest way we can find to satisfy ourselves.

If you are *not* in business for that reason, you are simply wasting your time. The wear and tear isn't worth it. And if you *are* in it for that reason, you had better damn well recognize that everybody else is in it for the same selfish reason.

Their self-interest motives should be your basis for dealing with everyone in business.

When you ask someone to do something, recognize that he is asking himself, "What's in it for me?"

When you establish a group objective, bear in mind that each member of the group is asking the same question.

When something happens or changes in your company, you can be certain that, consciously or subconsciously, each person involved is asking himself, "How does this affect me?"

Self-interest is the single most pervasive force in business. Mishandled it can be deadly, for individuals and for a company. Left alone it just about balances itself out, doing as much damage as it does good. But channeled— properly channeled—coordinated, unified, steered, and harnessed, it becomes a powerful constructive force, unifying people behind common goals, motivating them, releasing a great flow of creativity. Coordinated self-interest has, in fact, made American business the most massively productive and creative force in the world.

You can use either the negative or positive power of personal self-interest.

One sales manager asked the company president, "What reward can we offer our sales force to motivate them to meet this year's quota?"

The president's answer: "Tell them the ones who meet the quota get to keep their jobs."

That is the negative approach. It is used all the time in business. You and I are constantly being threatened by the loss of our job, our security, our status, the boss's approval, a customer's continued goodwill, a valued subordinate, or the freedom to do our work without more rules and regulations being loaded on us. It is this fear or negative force that helps to keep us on our toes. It keeps us from getting sloppy.

The positive side of self-interest, however, makes this negative side look anemic. Give people a chance to get big rewards that will satisfy their own personal hungers and you will cut loose such a positive force that you will think you have split an atom. The man who learns to accept individual self-interest as an unavoidable reality, to understand its dynamics, and to weld it into teamwork is the man most likely to succeed in business. He is the man most likely to satisfy his own personal self-interest.

All the good things and all the bad things about business flow from the natural human characteristic of self-interest.

Without the self-interest of business people, there would be no crooked deals, treachery, employee theft, obsession with wealth, boss-employee rivalries, sweatshops, cheating, or strikes.

But without personal self-interest, business would not be the productive, rewarding, enriching, satisfying, life-giving force that it is.

It is the big rewards that attract to business the strongest, smartest, most interesting, most highly motivated people.

But don't you forget for one minute that each one of them is in it for his own personal gain—not to help you succeed, not to help the company succeed, but to succeed himself.

**Everybody's motives are different.
Make certain you know what motivates
each person you deal with.**

People work for the strangest reasons. It takes a lot
more than money to make most people in business tick.

Each of us works in the way we do because of a
whole assortment of desires, needs, and ambitions. The
variety of things that motivate people is almost unlimited.

Some that may seem silly to you are very big in someone else's mind.

Every day much of what you do and say in your job brushes against the motives of the people you work with. You either contribute to or conflict with the forces that make them go. Sometimes conflicts can't be avoided but at least you should know what you are doing.

It would be great if you just had to remember that people are self-interested. Then it would be simple to mold individuals into perfectly coordinated teams for powerful, single-minded group action aimed at a specific worthwhile goal.

Unfortunately it is not that simple. You need to know what *kinds* of self-interest each individual is working to satisfy. You need to understand specifically what unique combination of motives makes each individual do what he is doing now in the way he is doing it. And you need to understand what nerves you can touch that will make him want to do what you want him to do in the way you want him to do it.

You destroy a person's value if you inadvertently thwart his basic motivation. But you turn him on if you help him satisfy his basic motivations.

There are certain assumptions you can make about what people want from their jobs. Just about everybody works in part for money, praise, pride in accomplishment, and because working in business is socially acceptable. From there on, though, motivations begin to splinter.

It would take the rest of the pages in this book just to list all of the types, varieties, styles, colors, and sub-categories of things that cause business people to work. Here is a random sample:

TANGIBLE REWARDS
>Money or its equivalent
>>For some people money is no motivation at all after they have satisfied today's immediate needs. For others money loses its power to motivate after they have achieved a certain level of comfort. And, of course, some will tear themselves apart with a lifetime of endless work to accumulate as much wealth as they can.

EGO SATISFACTION
>Status, or maybe just status symbols
>Reputation, or just reflected glory
>>Some people work because it puts them in touch with glorious people or a glorious company.
>Admiration, or at least respect from their peers
>Prestige and fame
>Titles
>Need for approval
>To prove they can do it
>To overcome feelings of inferiority

SOCIAL CONTACTS
>Camaraderie and friendship
>To overcome loneliness
>Contact with stimulating people
>Opportunity for gossip
>>The value of a job to some people is that it provides them with things to complain about and an audience to complain to.
>Contact with prospective husbands or wives

CREATIVE EXPRESSION
>Something interesting to do
>Pride in accomplishment

Personal growth and development
Self-expression
Curiosity

> This is one reason most people consider it a
> plum to have a job that involves travel to inter-
> esting places. Status is another.

AGGRESSION OR COMPETITIVE AMBITION
One-upmanship
Rivalry, or the need to excel
Vengeance, or to punish others
To prove others wrong
Winning, or the sport of it

ESCAPE
To escape from their problems

> For many people, working in business is a dis-
> traction that keeps their minds off their prob-
> lems, worries, aches and pains, and sadness.

To escape from social pressure
Noninvolvement

> Some people, especially women, go to business
> so they won't have to get involved in other
> activities, like changing diapers or attending
> garden-club meetings.

A place to go

> Some people go to work—and enjoy staying
> late—to get away from someplace worse—
> like home.

To avoid punishment
To escape controls, rules, or restrictions

> For example, the president of a small company
> may work hard at good employee relations to
> avoid the restrictions of being unionized.

Laziness

>This is a strong and little-understood motivation. Some people work very hard and creatively because they really despise work and are trying to get free of it. A paradox.

To escape the possibility of failure

To escape feelings of guilt for not working

Path of least resistance

>For some people, working in business is just the normal thing to do. They literally cannot think of any alternatives.

To escape boredom

>This is one of the biggest reasons people work. Ask anyone who has been out of a job for a while, or retired.

COMFORT

Security

Routine

>There can be a lot of comfort in a rut.

Habit or conditioned reflexes

An enjoyable life style

Pleasant working conditions

Available sex opportunities

DUTY

Mature feelings of responsibility

Self-punishment

>"In the sweat of thy face shalt thou eat bread . . ."

Self-image

>Some people work at a particular job in a particular way because it's the way their father did it.

For noble reasons . . .

> . . . like contributing to the well-being of mankind, aiding in the national defense, making a better world. There is some of this in most of us, but the people who work in business for noble reasons alone can be counted on the fingers of one hand.

PERSONALITY QUIRKS

Destructive urges

Mystical reasons

> It is surprising how many people run their business lives by "voices," superstition, and compulsion. One respected management consultant admitted in a weak moment that many of his business actions, and some of the high-priced advice he gives his corporate clients, are based on his horoscope in the daily newspaper.

This list could have been constructed in order of importance, on the basis of a statistical study on what makes most people work. That, however, would defeat your purpose. You are concerned not with quantified generalities but with the unique combination of motives of Bob, Tom, Sally, Gertrude, Shadrach, and the other individuals you work with.

It is up to you to identify the motives of each of these individuals and rank them in order of importance to him or her.

You will probably find that a person's various motives are interwoven into an intricate pattern. Usually, however, you find that the pattern is dominated by primary or special motives. There may be only two or three of these and they are the ones you should pay most attention to, without ignoring the others.

Sometimes it is easy to identify a person's motives, sometimes not so easy. People have secret needs and desires they may not admit even to themselves. The fact that a person is ashamed of his motives does not change the fact that they are a powerful part of his life.

If you can get an insight into a person's hidden but true motives without offending him, you have the key to unlocking his full potential.

You don't have to be a psychologist to accomplish this. All you need to do is look and listen carefully—mostly listen.

Some people state their motives openly and directly. Others reveal them indirectly or unconsciously. A person whose conversation contains repeated references to money is probably highly motivated by money. Someone who is hung up on titles is probably motivated by the need for ego satisfaction.

One point to keep in mind: people's motives change, particularly as their situations change. As motives are satisfied, others become dominant. Once an ego-driven person gets that big title and a corner office, the desire for more leisure may become his chief motivating force.

Unless other people's motives are satisfied while you are satisfying your own, your success is going to be limited at best.

Ignore the motives of others and you give them no reason to help you satisfy yours.

Don't bother to understand the motives of the other guy and you will probably frustrate him and tramp on his toes—without realizing the damage you are doing.

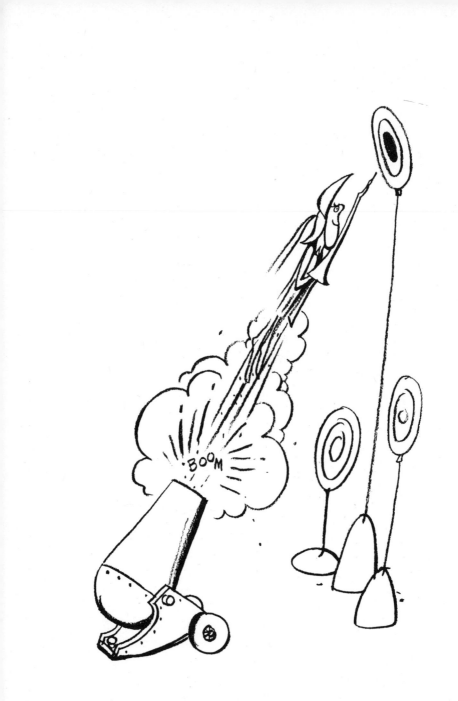

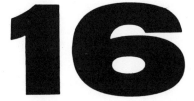

16

Know exactly what your goals are.

Goal setting is one of the skills that most directly determine your success.

You simply cannot get far in business without purposeful goals. You can't even plan your strategy.

You will probably accomplish most of what you set

as reasonable goals. Therefore, you might as well set your targets high enough to mean something.*

The reason most people in business flounder is that they are goal-less. They have no personal goals at all, or their goals are undefined, too easy, or not worth the effort.

Could this be you:

A young guy starts his career lean and hungry, working to eat. Years roll by, he puts on a layer of fat and accumulates some success. Now he works for new reasons: comfort and status, for example. More years go by and he is still working—but now he has forgotten why. He goes to the office at the same time everyday. He makes the same kinds of telephone calls, writes the same kinds of memos, eats the same kinds of lunches with the same kinds of people, and reads the same business publications.

We ask this aging fellow why he does it and all we get is a quizzical look or an embarrassed laugh. The truth is he doesn't know why. He has worked all his life, that's all. His only goal is to retire. His job has become an ingrained habit. Sad.

Have you ever thought of writing the story of the rest of your life? It's a great way to learn things about yourself and your goals. Turn your imagination loose but don't write a fairy tale; write an honest account of how you would most like your life to unfold. Don't stop at age sixty-five; assume you are going to live to be eighty-five or ninety, and take the story to the end.

* Henry David Thoreau said it in *Walden:* "In the long run men hit only what they aim at. Therefore, though they should fail immediately they had better aim at something high."

Start by asking yourself: Why am I working? What do I want? What are the things I want most to accomplish? Where am I headed? Where should I be headed? When I get there am I going to be satisfied?

If you are married, ask your wife or husband to write a version of your life story, for comparison purposes.

The insights that come from this exercise will startle you. You will get a fresh new perspective on what your real goals are—or ought to be.

The most alive, interesting, successful people in business—of every age—are the ones with the clearest focus on their personal and business goals. Ask a man in this category what his goals are and he will probably tell you in no uncertain terms.

"Today," he might say, "my goal is to finish my report on the Scovill account. By the end of the week I want to get one of three possible new accounts signed up so I can relax for the weekend and take my boy fishing. This month I want to add one more good man to my staff. By the end of the year I want to show a 30 percent increase over what we did last year. In five years I want to be president of the company. In ten years I want to be able to quit so I can go back to school, get another degree, and teach in a little college I have picked out in Maine."

Notice that this man's goals are specific, with deadlines. Deadlines are what give your goals teeth. Goals without deadlines are mere wishful thinking.

Notice also that this man's goals are both short range and long range. At all times he knows precisely what he is working for. As a result, everything he does is likely to fit into a purposeful, harmonious pattern.

Will things work out for this fellow in line with his goals? Probably not, for two reasons.

First, he is matching his goals against conditions that are changing or unknown to him. Somebody else may have hired the man he aims to hire; somebody else may also have set the presidency as his goal.

Second, the man's own goals will change, as will yours over a period of time. He will change them in line with changing conditions. And he will change them as his own values change. Some of his goals will be met and passed; others will be altered; and others will be abandoned and replaced.

With goals such as this man has set, it is predictable that the changes he makes in his goals will be upward. He will probably accomplish most of what he sets out to accomplish faster than he thought he could.

How high should your goals be? The best goal is well beyond your present reach, yet still in view.

Don't just set a deadline for the final goal; set deadlines for each intermediate step. That forces you to translate your goals into plans and strategy. When you have done that, you are halfway there already.

It is smart to let people know what your goals are. This helps to solidify your goals and commit you to what you say you are going to do. Equally important, it eliminates misunderstandings.

As an experiment, ask some of your associates to tell you what they think your goals are. Chances are the feedback will not always agree with what you think your goals are. Who is wrong, you or they? If they are wrong, what misleading signals are you giving? If you are wrong, then why have you been telling yourself all this time that you have been working for reasons other than your true reasons?

Goal setting means also setting priorities—forward and back. There are going to be lean times in your career as well as lush. To prepare for these one-step-forward-two-steps-back periods, know what you can give up and what you can't.

About a year ago I was forced to assess my personal priorities. My business had suffered a series of setbacks; it looked like all I had built over a ten-year period might tumble.

My wife and I worked out a two-sided priority list. First we made a "retreat" list—the ranked order of things we were prepared to give up as a means of protecting the things we would not give up. To balance that list, we listed all the things we wanted to do and acquire when my personal economic barometer began to rise again. This list was lifelong in scope.

It is interesting to look at the list now. In a year's time, we have already attained about half the goals we set for our lifetime. Most of the other goals have become very real likelihoods for the next few years at most.

Clearly, I need a whole new set of goals.

Think about it. Maybe you do too.

**Surprise is a powerful tactic.
Use it carefully. It can be disastrous.**

Nobody in business likes to be surprised.

There is good reason; in business, surprise usually means trouble.

Surprise! "We're transferring you to Nome, Charlie. Can you and your family be ready to leave next week?"

Surprise! "Before you cover your typewriter, Miss Brown, I'll need this forty-page report first thing in the morning."

Surprise! "I quit."

Surprise! "You see, my brother-in-law set up a company to make a product like yours and. . . ."

Surprise! "While you were on vacation we moved Steve into your office. This map will help you find where we put your desk and things."

Surprise! "I have called you all together to tell you that. . . ."

Surprises are fine for your wife on your anniversary or your kids at Christmas, but in business, avoid them.

Most people you work with don't like changes of any kind. They especially don't like to be caught off guard or off balance. They don't like a sudden change that comes without warning.

A surprise may mean an accident has happened. It may mean a competitor has caught you napping. It may mean things have been developing around you that you should have known about but didn't.

Surprise may also mean that someone is using devious methods to win a tactical advantage over you or someone else. Surprise *is* a powerful tactic. That is why it is so frequently used and why you may be tempted to use it.

Playing with surprises can be like playing with firecrackers. A good surprise explodes with the same satisfying impact as a firecracker. But people who play with firecrackers and people who play with surprises run the same risk: some carry the scars or disabilities of their miscalculations for life.

The basic tactic of surprise is simple. You put a

certain change in motion that will affect another person. But you withhold from him some or all of the information about the change. Then, when it is too late for him to take evasive action or countermeasures, you open the floodgates of the informational dam and overpower him.

Good timing is essential, of course, in bringing off a good surprise. You can only dam the natural flow of information so long before a leak will occur (see Rule 10). On the other hand, the more information you hold back, the bigger the surprise.

Surprise is a wholly acceptable tactic for competing companies to use against each other. Without it there would be a lot less competition. It keeps competition wholesome, healthy, and invigorating.

Intercompany surprise, therefore, is good for business as a whole.

Intracompany surprise is a different matter. When surprise is used within a company by one individual or group against another individual or group, it is seldom positive or productive. Quite the opposite; it tends to be destructive in several ways.

Mutual trust is essential in successful business, and surprise undermines trust. If you surprise me I may never quite trust you again. I'm going to protect myself against the possibility that you have another surprise up your sleeve. In fact, I'll probably assume that you do.

In business there is a huge difference between an opponent and an enemy, particularly a bitter enemy. When you have a worthy opponent, or a rival, you and he are playing the game of business, presumably with some semblance of chivalry. When your opponent becomes an enemy, the game turns to war. Sometimes it is the tactic of surprise that polarizes a latent rival into an enemy.

Your surprise elicits a bigger one in response, and the war is on. That could mean disaster for either of you, or maybe both of you.

Inadvertent, unintentional, or miscalculated surprises are usually more destructive than planned ones; they are certainly just as dangerous.

An unintentional surprise is usually caused by a breakdown in communications—one of the biggest problems in business. If you are contributing to a communications breakdown in your company, you ought to think about what it is costing. And you ought to be on your guard for the backlash.

Example.

The sales manager suddenly discovers that the production manager has added a better whammy to the number one product line. Great! Wonderful! Terrific! Big surprise! Except that it doesn't help sales when the sales force doesn't know about it. And it doesn't contribute to the sales manager's opinion of the production manager when the production manager doesn't tell the sales manager what the sales manager needs to know.

Communications breakdown can be the scourge of any organization. Top people fail to communicate down. Bottom people fail to communicate up. People on the same level fail to communicate across. In some companies the result is that it is not just a matter of the right hand not knowing what the left is doing. It is so bad that the first finger doesn't know what the second finger on the same hand is doing. And when that situation exists, you have unpleasant surprises popping up all over the place.

The president doesn't know that the main production line has been down for three hours.

The branch manager doesn't know there has been a reorganization at headquarters and now he reports to Roscoe instead of Conrad.

The receptionist doesn't know the ad manager will be in Europe for two weeks.

The bookkeeper doesn't know the deadline for his report has been moved up.

All surprises. All unintentional. All counter-effective.

Even good news sometimes comes as a surprise. Not often, but sometimes. Good things that happen in business are usually well heralded and impatiently awaited. They are usually so late they are anything but surprises.

Thus, when you have even good news coming as a surprise to people in your organization, you know you have a critical case of communications breakdown.

Remember these three things about surprises:

First, people want to know exactly where they stand with you, where you stand, and what gives. They want the news as soon as possible. They don't want to be kidded or fooled. They don't want any surprises. If you surprise someone, he may use his position or power to surprise you back—by keeping you in the dark, or inflicting a sudden change on you without warning.

Second, you can avoid causing surprises by keeping all your channels of communication open—through conscious effort—and by considering the interests of others when some new development happens.

Third, the worst kind of surprise is the surprise you cause for yourself. By being unprepared. By being uninformed. By failing to analyze the probable outcome of a situation.

In business, change is essential, but sudden change without warning can be devastating.

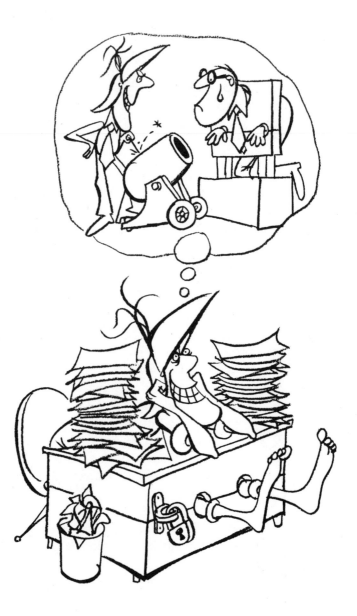

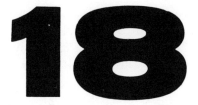

**Revenge is sweet but it is God's
privilege, not yours.**

Picture your worst enemy.

Think how satisfying it would be to bash the guy's brains in.

Now, having savored in your imagination the satisfaction of revenge, forget it.

You can't be successful in business if you squander your time and energy thinking up ways to get even with people.

It isn't a matter of morality; it's a matter of practicality. Revenge is ineffective. It doesn't work. If it contributed to your success, that would be one thing. But it doesn't. So forget it.

Revenge may damage your enemies, but it also damages you, maybe more. It doesn't do your reputation any good. It may cause people to fear you, but who needs that?

Think of the wear and tear of revenge. When your blood boils and your system is full of adrenaline, you are killing yourself. Sometimes the worst thing an enemy can do to you is cause you to lose your cool and respond wildly. Why give him that satisfaction?

Revenge lets an enemy know he has hurt you, and if you seek revenge on him, he may seek greater revenge on you. This means more damage and more time spent defending yourself instead of moving forward. If you respond again in kind, the war is on. Nobody wins wars.

Revenge costs too much. It lowers you to the level of your enemies whose tactics you are copying. It is inconclusive.

There are far more effective ways to deal with your enemies in business. The technique or combination of techniques you should use depends on what kind of enemy you are dealing with. What you do to an enemy should depend a lot on whether it is his fault or your fault that he got that way.

These are your primary choices:

1. *Turn your back on him.* Nothing defeats a serious

enemy more than not taking his attacks seriously. Show him that you consider his actions childish, not worthy of your attention. No one likes to be cast in the role of a fool. If you successfully cast an enemy in that role, it may cause him to alter his actions toward you to avoid proving you right.

Be careful about which enemies you turn your back on. Miscalculate and you could wind up with a knife between your shoulder blades.

2. *Neutralize him.* Create a defense to blunt his attacks. If he is spreading false rumors, broadcast the facts. If he is trying to get others to ally themselves with him against you, win these people as your own allies. If your enemy knows your weakness and is attacking you there, correct your weakness, compensate for it, or get someone else to support you who is strong where you are weak.

3. *Make a truce.* This simply means that you agree not to hurt him if he agrees not to hurt you. You can tacitly show your willingness for a truce by your actions or you can sit down face to face, recognize the problems that exist between you, and hammer out a treaty. Better yet, make an agreement to support each other.

4. *Turn him into a friend.* This is an extension of making a truce. Convince your enemy that if you have the power to hurt each other, you undoubtedly have the power to help each other too. Figure out what self-interest of his you are able to serve, and approach him from that direction.

5. *Gain a better strategic position.* Put yourself out of your enemy's reach. There is a reason why some ancient cities were built on hilltops: it made it difficult for

enemies to attack. The more costly or difficult you make it for an enemy to succeed in attacking you, the less likely it is he will try, and thus the less likely he will remain in the active role of an enemy. How you get out of his reach is for you to work out.

6. *If he insists on defeating himself, let him.* Some enemies just can't be turned off or pacified. These are usually people with personal problems that they feel compelled to exorcise by acting out aggressions toward someone. If such a person picks you as that unlucky someone, there isn't much you can do except stay out of range. Those destructive urges may well be self-destructive in origin. Unless you can relieve that person's psychological anguish, which is unlikely, your best bet is to hold your ground and let the attacker wear himself out. At that point, having failed to shake you seriously, he will almost always remove himself from the scene, or be removed. The damage done by a self-destructive enemy can usually be controlled and held to a minimum.

7. *Refuse to treat him like an enemy.* Most people in business tend to behave the way they are expected to behave. Treat a man like a dope and he will probably act like a dope. Treat him like a responsible, worthy person and he will tend to behave like one.

If you treat an enemy like an enemy, he will almost certainly act like an enemy, but if you don't treat him like an enemy, or don't even recognize him as such, he will be uncomfortable about treating you like an enemy, and may even stop.

This is a good strategy to use on an enemy whose position is superior to yours or who has more power than you do. After all, what choice have you got?

8. *Outsucceed him.* Put your fight on a positive basis rather than a negative basis. Instead of tripping him up or worrying about him tripping you up, outpace him in the race for success. If you get far enough ahead of him, he can't hurt you. If he wants to waste his ammunition taking potshots at you, let him.

What better way is there to treat your enemies than to leave them behind?

9. *Remove the reason why your enemy hates you.* This is the most obvious technique of all, yet it is often overlooked and neglected. That's because you have to start by admitting that you have the power to correct the problem, which probably indicates that you caused the problem in the first place, or helped to cause it.

If you were wrong or are wrong, admit it to your enemy. Apologize openly, no matter how much it hurts and no matter how much damage he has done to you. To the best of your ability, correct the mistake you made that turned him into an enemy. Then if he continues as an enemy, at least he won't get much support; people will know his attitude toward you now is unjustified.

Properly used, these techniques of dealing with enemies are more conclusive, more satisfying, and more self-serving than revenge. They don't have any of the backlash or other self-damaging effects that revenge has.

All these techniques, however, require one basic quality on your part: patience. If you are like most success-seeking people in business, you are congenitally impatient. To deal successfully with your enemies you must hold your impatience in check.

Relax. Act sensibly, be patient, reject revenge—and you will win.

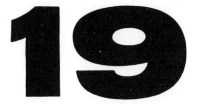

**Enemies are a fact of life, but
a few are plenty.**

You can make a good guess at how successful a man
will be if you know who his enemies are. For example,
his success is in doubt if—

- He has been in business several years and has no
  enemies.

- He has a large number of enemies.
- He has enemies that he is not aware of.
- His enemies are people with whom he has been dishonest.
- His enemies include people in positions of power higher than his own.

On the other hand, bet on him to succeed if—

- He has been in business several years and has just a few enemies.
- He has unmasked his secret and latent enemies.
- His enemies are people whose power to hurt him is limited.
- His enemies are people who have tried but failed to compromise him.

What this boils down to is that you can judge a man not only by the company he keeps but by the enemies he makes.

A business enemy is a friend or adversary turned sour. He is as interested in punishing you as he is in rewarding himself.

If you have no business enemies, you may be a diplomatic genius or kidding yourself. More likely, you are pussyfooting. You are going too slow. You are being too careful, taking too few or too small risks, operating in the protected but unrewarding areas of business instead of the more dangerous, adventurous areas where the big rewards are.

It is virtually impossible to accomplish anything worthwhile in business without creating enemies. You can't work at your full personal capacity or grow to your full stature without exposing yourself to enemy attack.

Enemies are dangerous and costly, but take your choice: succeed by dealing with them, or pacify them and settle for mediocrity.

Enemies are like weeds in a vegetable garden. If the soil is rich, the weeds flourish. If you want to harvest the crop, chop the weeds.

Unaware outsiders may look at business and be surprised that there is not more feuding, fussing, and fighting than there already is. They see organizations and individuals knocking their ideas together, their motives clashing, straining to outdo each other. They see union and management locked in battle, the veneer of politeness stripped off, the tough muscle of basic language and desperate tactics laid bare, but after the bargain is struck, both sides smile, shake hands, and usually mean it.

If this kind of combat doesn't make enemies, what does? The answer is that business enemies are conceived in four ways.

1. *Dishonesty creates enemies.* Honest competition does not make enemies; dishonest competition does. Think about it. How many situations do you know where the root reason for two people, two companies, or two countries hating each other is that one (or both) lied to, cheated on, stole from, or was otherwise dishonest with the other?

2. *Diplomatic mistakes create enemies.* Human beings are sensitive instruments burdened with a weight of pride. Our sensitized, antlike antennae extend out, probing for signals of approval or disapproval, respect

or disrespect, compliment or affront, acceptance or rejection, praise or blame, recognition or neglect. If we pick up negative signals or fail to pick up positive signals, our pride may become inflamed. Often meaningless static is decoded into an affront.

Damaging someone's pride is enough to crystalize his enmity.

Some people obviously are better diplomats than others. It seems virtually impossible, however, for anyone who really strives for success to avoid denting somebody's ego. Praise Oscar, and Joe is wounded. Point out an error to Harry, and he reads it as a calculated attack. Fail to glorify Gloria's work with superlatives, and she tells her husband you hate her; then both of them start hating you.

Sometimes it seems you could sit motionless, take no action, say nothing, let no expression appear on your face, and some idiot would get his feelings hurt.

It is like the classic joke: two psychiatrists pass on the street, both say "Hello," and then each thinks to himself, "I wonder what he meant by that!"

3. *Threats, real or imagined, create enemies.* Whereas it is virtually impossible for a success-seeking man to avoid insulting some people, it is *totally* impossible for him to avoid being a threat to some people.

You continually face situations where your success depends on change. But change creates threats—to other people's position, security, ease, or habit.

When you threaten someone, you may cause him to fight or flee. Either way, you may make an enemy. Sometimes just possessing the power to upset the status quo is enough to harden another person into an enemy—simply because you are a threat to him.

4. *Sticking to your guns creates enemies.* If you fail to satisfy people who try to compromise you, they may decide to destroy you. An employee may try to force you to lower your performance standards. Co-workers may try to get you to join them in some dishonest action. A superior may try to get you to compromise your loyalty to others by demanding that you give your loyalty only to him.

Believe it or not, some people in business consider it a personal insult if you fail to see things their way. It angers them and turns them into enemies, especially when you stand firm in the face of strong pressure to give in.

It should be clear by now that it is not just *what* you do but *how* you do it that creates enemies.

It should also be clear that there are different kinds of enemies: announced enemies, unannounced enemies, and secret enemies.

Announced enemies are the best kind. They are usually fairly honest about it. An announced enemy tells you that he hates your guts. Okay, you know where you stand with him and that you had better be on your guard for the worst.

Unannounced enemies are more dangerous. They don't try to disguise the fact that they are your enemy; they just don't bother to tell you. An unannounced enemy may catch you by surprise.

Secret enemies are the most dangerous of all. They work through subterfuge. A secret enemy is two-faced; he thinks his treacherous thoughts, spreads his venomous rumors, and then makes his destructive moves behind a mask of smiles, courtesy, respect, and friendliness. A secret enemy may lack the power to attack you head-on, but this does not diminish the danger. A secret enemy works insidiously, eating away at you in ways you may not see or feel until it is too late. Secret enemies are the ones who kill you.

It is easy to identify a secret enemy after it is too late. Your defense, however, depends on spotting him before he does his damage.

This can be tough. Sometimes the only way to do it is to analyze some special circumstances or examine mistakes you have made. Who has—or could have—misunderstood something you have said or done? Who has—or could have—been threatened by a change you have made? Who is living in fear of a change you could make? Who has been caught with his pants down—did you find out about something that was supposed to be kept a secret?

You probably get a regular medical checkup to keep tabs on your physical problems and to make sure your body contains no secret disease. If you are wise, you give your business life the same kind of regular checkup. It is a way to keep tabs on your overt enemies and search for symptoms that could signal the presence of hidden enemies.

As in medicine, preventing the problem is usually better than dealing with it later. If you can avoid making an enemy you may save yourself a lot of time and grief.

There are times, however, when it costs less in the long run to have an enemy than to avoid one.

Don't be afraid to make enemies when the alternative is to sell yourself out. Compromise is essential for business success, but there are times to compromise and times not to. Don't compromise yourself or your company when the cost of compromise is more than the cost of making an enemy.

Let's face it. You lose support by making enemies. But sometimes you gain more support than you lose— by openly and completely opposing another individual or group. It helps if you are right and they are wrong.

You can have a lot of enemies and still be highly successful. The only trouble is that you will probably be so wounded and crippled you can't enjoy it.

Never make a decision until you have to.

You get a lot of advice on being decisive.

You know it is virtuous to make courageous decisions based on solid facts. You know that once you make a decision you should not vacillate. Et cetera.

What you don't hear about is that people in business

make too many decisions too soon. Or in the wrong sequence.

Every decision you make is a compromise. It costs you something, maybe plenty. It means giving up your options and alternatives. A decision to do something is really a decision not to do everything else. Why make a commitment like that before there is a reason to?

Decision making is what business is all about. How well you do it determines how far you go, and where. That goes for the small, everyday decisions as well as the big, strategic ones.

People in business face a never-ending series of forks in the road. If you decide now about a fork you won't reach until later, you cheat yourself. You have canceled your chance to take any of the intersections, crossroads, or possible shortcuts you will pass between here and there.

New opportunities present themselves all the time, but usually suddenly. If you decide things too soon you lose the flexibility to grab the opportunities that keep coming up.

The solution is to make tentative decisions in advance, otherwise known as a game plan. It is great to know where you want to go and how you think you can get there. But keep your plans broad and flexible rather than narrow and confining. Make sure your plan contains lots of options, and know what they are. Don't eliminate any alternatives—no matter how clearly your plan seems to be carrying you in a specific direction—until you actually reach the fork in the road and must decide.

For one thing, it gives you bargaining power to keep your alternative courses of action clear. If you approach a decision point having left yourself no choice but to go one way, you have given up the strength of a possible advantage.

Suppose, for example, you are interviewing candidates for a job. You narrow the choice down to Tom, Dick, and Harry, all good men, but decide that Dick is your man. You thank Tom and Harry and tell them you have found a man who is a little better qualified for the job.

Then you offer Dick the job. He says he would like to accept if you will raise the pay 10 percent over what you are offering. Too bad. You have already kissed off your alternatives. It is either give the man what he wants or back to the drawing board.

Or turn the situation around. You are being interviewed for a job that is a real plum. You want it so badly you can taste it. They tell you you've got the inside track; it will just be a matter of time before the hiring authorization comes through. You tell your wife and friends you have a new job. To be fair, you even tell your boss to start looking for a replacement. Then you get the word: the hiring authorization came through all right, but at a much lower salary level. Do you still want the job? At this point you probably have no choice but to take it.

Making decisions too soon is not just a matter of poor strategy. Things change. They change in ways no one can foresee. A good manager plans for his company's future needs. But preplanning and predeciding are two different things. The longer you wait before making a decision, the more facts you are likely to have to work with.

Let's say a president and his board of directors see

the need for a new plant in five years. They buy a piece of land, commission an architect, get the zoning and other legal requirements cleaned up, sign an agreement with an investment bank to raise the necessary money, and sign up a contractor who agrees to complete the plant by a certain date at a certain cost.

The president and board congratulate themselves on the astute decisions they have made to put the company in position to reap its future rewards.

Then several things happen. Land adjacent to the present plant becomes available because the cantankerous old farmer who owned it has finally died. A new kind of building material becomes available that could permit a cheaper design for the plant—but the architect's design is already frozen. Then, just before construction begins, the economy slumps. Construction prices drop—but the company is already committed to a contractor. Further, because of the slump, the underwriter cannot raise as much money as is needed. And anyway, it now appears that the new plant won't be needed so soon after all.

A ridiculous example? Of course. But people in business know these things happen everyday. Why? Because too many decisions are made too soon.

Often when you face a big decision you find you can easily break it down into small decisions. Most of these can be put off until later. This keeps you loose.

Make decisions—final decisions, that is—only when you have reached the point where you must actually go one way or another. Then try to pick a route that takes you in the direction of your overall goal, but that also will present you with a continuing choice of alternative routes or options as you move along.

Nothing is worse than to make a beeline for the end of the rainbow only to find that the pot of gold has been moved somewhere else.

Yes, there is one thing worse. It is to make a beeline for your preselected objective only to find you are on a dead end that doesn't go quite that far.

The worst kind of decision is the decision to retreat from a decision you have already made. The best way to avoid this costly process is to plan your decisions with care, know what your options are and where they will lead, and avoid making your decisions too soon.

Notice we are not even talking about making decisions too late. If you don't know it already, you can guess what kind of disaster that brings.

Follow your own instincts. They are probably no more wrong than everyone else's carefully reasoned logic.

It takes more than facts to make a decision. A decision's quality depends on what you add to the facts.

You can take a sack of flour and turn it into biscuits or cake. It depends on the other ingredients. And the cook.

You can take a set of facts and turn them into subsistence or a profit. It depends on the other ingredients. And the decision maker.

Most of the working material that exists in your mind cannot be expressed in words or numbers. It consists of feelings, fears, beliefs, doubts, prejudices, and convictions, all stemming from unremembered experiences. It is your subconscious. Some call it instinct or intuition. It doesn't matter what you call it. The point is that this unexpressible part of you is what determines the quality of your decisions. If you haven't learned to release it and use it, start learning.

People in business argue whether business is an art or a science. It is both. It is a science because you have to stick to the facts. But if that were all, computers could make all our business decisions for us. It is an art because the value of each decision is determined by the creative interpretation of the decider. As in other forms of art, there is sometimes only a thin line between a good decision and a bad one.

The problem in decision making is that there are never enough facts. If you had all the facts, it wouldn't be a decision; it would be a foregone conclusion. If you have no facts you can't make a decision; you can only make a shot in the dark.

Decision making implies limited or incomplete facts. It is how you organize the facts and what you add to fill the gaps that reveal your talent as a decision maker.

Of course, the more facts you have, the better. Everybody knows that the first step in decision making is to get the facts. That may be the biggest part of the job, but it is what you do with the facts that really counts.

People being what they are, facts get interpreted differently. How *you* interpret a set of facts is what distinguishes you from other people. And that is why making your own decisions is important.

In business you are not always in a position to make your own decisions. But if a decision concerns you, make it yourself, if you can. Get the facts, listen to everybody's advice, but make the decision yourself. You are the one who has to live with it. If you let others make it, the decision will be right for them, but maybe not so right for you.

If you are responsible for a certain area of work, try to make or control the decisions that relate to your work. You are going to be the guy who has to carry out the decision. It is much easier, more satisfying, and usually more results-producing to carry out a decision you have shaped and shaded than one someone else hands to you.

Keep one thing in mind: if you don't make the decisions that are yours to make, somebody else will.

Decisiveness is an ability that comes naturally to some people but has to be learned by others. The most valuable men and women in business are those who can make decisions easily, quickly, and convincingly.

If a decision is tough, it usually means one of two things. Either you don't have enough facts or the decision is not being made in the context of a good plan.

To win in business you only have to be right 51 percent of the time. The big rewards come, however, when your decisions are consistent, most of them are right, and some of them are innovative.

You can't make innovative decisions with just facts.

**Build a reputation as a winner by
smiling when you win—and when you lose.**

Business is populated by winners, losers, and mediocrities.

There is no point talking about the mediocrities. They are dull. They seldom win and they seldom lose. They just plod along. How boring.

Losers are more interesting, and winners are far more interesting.

Winners and losers have many traits in common. In fact, some people in business never learn to distinguish them. This includes some wise old executives in major corporations who are repeatedly hoodwinked by losers.

The reason is that some losers take on the convincing coloration of winners. By acting like winners they get treated like winners.

There is a lesson here for you: if you are a winner you had damn well better act like one. If you don't, some loser is going to come along and take your winnings.

When you blow all the smoke away, there are two main things that determine whether a man will be a winner or a loser in business.

The first is his style of winning and losing.

The second is the pattern of his victories and defeats.

Don't think it is a matter of talent. Some of the most talented people in business are losers because they don't develop a winning style or a consistent pattern in their victories. You know from experience that some of the least talented people walk off with the biggest prizes.

You cannot win all of your battles in business. Paradoxically, to be a winner it sometimes seems as if you have to lose more times than you win.

A winner loses in a different way from a loser.

A winner never permits a defeat to become decisive. He may retreat, but he doesn't submit. When he loses, his style is to create the impression that he has experienced only a temporary and minor delay in his inevitable victory.

A loser thinks of his losses as disasters. He is easily

devastated. He suffers a loss poorly. For him a loss is indeed a setback. It destroys him. It forces him to lose his foothold and slide backward. It takes something away from him, temporarily or maybe even permanently.

Just as a winner loses in a different way from a loser, a loser wins in a different way from a winner.

When a winner wins, he gives the impression that the outcome is exactly what he expected, which it probably was. He treats winning as normal. He is pleased, of course, but he responds to his victory calmly, especially since he is busy planning his next victory.

The loser, on the other hand, is often surprised, even amazed by his victory. He is more likely to sponsor a big celebration when things go right. By his reaction to winning, he indicates that he really didn't expect to win. He indicates that he is more accustomed to losing.

Winners and losers establish different kinds of patterns for their victories and defeats.

Losers are less selective in the battles they start. They often start things where they are bound to lose, or where they cannot win big. If they thought about it in advance, they would see that they were going to get beaten, or bested, or compromised.

A winner is more circumspect in selecting the battles he will fight. He undertakes only those where (a) the odds are in his favor, (b) the cost of losing is not great, or (c) the rewards of winning are worth the risk even if winning is a long shot. He thoughtfully balances the risk with the probable or possible result.

This does not mean the winner fails to take chances. He takes plenty of chances. That is how he gets his reputation as a winner. But his risks are calculated risks.

not foolish risks, as is often the case with losers. A winner takes risks only when he is confident he can handle the resulting success or the resulting failure.

A loser fails to calculate either. Thus, he not only loses when he loses; he often loses when he wins because he doesn't know what to do with his victory. For him, winning the wrong kind of victory may be worse than not having won at all.

A winner's battles and therefore his victories tend to be consistent with each other. They fall into a pattern. Each victory sets the stage for the next. The winner moves ahead in a planned direction.

In contrast, a loser's victories are scattered, random, and inconsistent. A loser may win more often than a winner, but the value of his winnings is less, or useless, because his victories don't add up. They do not form a pattern. More likely, it is his losses that form a predictable pattern.

Until now your career has unquestionably been marbled by a combination of victories and defeats. Some of your defeats have been caused by mistakes you have made. Some have been caused by risks you have taken. Some have been caused by changing conditions that you failed to—or were unable to—respond to. Some have been caused by the fact that other people let you down.

Your working life will continue to be marked by a combination of winnings and losses. The thing that will determine whether you are a winner or loser is not whether you experience victories or defeats, but how you handle both.

Of course, there is the essential requirement of

making certain that your victories, on balance, outweigh your defeats.

But just as there is obviously something wrong if your defeats outnumber your victories, too many victories can also indicate something is wrong. If you win too often, it means you have set your sights too low. That is no way to become a true winner.

Think of some people you know in business. Why do you think of one person as a winner and another as a loser? Isn't your opinion of each at least partly determined by his opinion of himself? A man in business builds a reputation as a winner by acting like a winner. That behavior of his, and the reputation that results, helps to make him a winner. Even when he is a winner, he will sometimes lose. If he starts acting like a loser, people will think of him as a loser, and treat him like a loser. That will help to make him a loser.

The way to be successful, and stay that way, is to act like a winner regardless of whether, at the moment, you happen to be winning or losing.

If you are in a job where winning and losing don't mean anything, you have my sympathy. Too bad. You are missing the excitement of business. No wonder you are bored stiff. If your energies have already drained away and your spirit has atrophied, stay put and make the best of a bad situation. But if there is still a chance you can revive, get yourself back in trim and enjoy the stimulation of being challenged, then get the hell out of that dull job and get into one where you can win and lose.

**Keep every promise you have made—
or that others think you have made.**

Two people shake hands, actually or figuratively, and you have a business deal—or do you?

More likely, you have two deals: (1) the deal that is understood by the party of the first part, and (2) the deal that is understood by the party of the second part.

In short order, the deal gets out of hand and develops some new twists. First there is the deal each man tells his wife he made, which is to say, the deal he wishes he had made. Then there is the deal he realizes he should have made, the deal he tries to convince himself he did make, and the deal he tries to convince the other fellow he made.

If each man in this deal satisfies the terms of it in line with his own interpretation of it, chances are one or the other is going to feel he got gypped.

And there you have one of the stickiest problems of business. The vast majority of everyday business promises neglect more essential points than they cover. They leave too much room for misunderstanding.

You hear a lot about big deals in business. Little deals, however, are much more important. The reason is that there are so many more little deals than big deals, and so many more people involved.

Every day, people in business make millions of promises: promises to pay . . . promises to deliver . . . promises to meet deadlines . . . promises to take action B if someone else takes action A . . . promises to perform in the other person's absence the way you perform in his presence . . . promises to follow rules and procedures. These promises are the threads that weave business together. Too bad so many of them are frayed, tangled, knotted, short, and broken. Too bad so many business promises are sloppy, insufficient, weak, and wasteful.

One reason for the problem is that the same words don't always mean the same things to different people— especially the way businessmen use and misuse language.

Another problem is that people don't listen to each other. Another is that they honestly forget. Another is that they don't express everything they are thinking. Another is that they do not know how to say clearly what they think.

We all view our promises through the tinted glasses of our own personal self-interest. No matter how hard you try to be objective, you hear what you like to hear and don't hear what you don't like to hear. What you think someone said or implied or promised or meant may not be what he said, implied, promised, or meant at all.

Most people in business don't make a habit of breaking promises. But we all do, sometime or other, give ground to the temptation to bend our promises, or mold them, to better fit our own interests.

It is the ambiguities of business promises, and their unintentional or intentional misinterpretations, that cause the most trouble. Look at all the time spent clearing up misunderstandings.

Example.

Fritz the production manager telephones Kurt the purchasing agent.

FRITZ: I'm going to need a thousand extra J-64 components for the Skasafram production line. Gotta have them next week.

KURT: Okay, I'll see what I can do.

FRITZ: Okay, but I gotta have them next week.

Next Monday arrives and Fritz again calls Kurt.

FRITZ: Where are my J-64s?

KURT: I hope to have them here Friday.

FRITZ: Friday! I told you I needed them today.

KURT: I told you I'd do my best for this week. Maybe they will be here Thursday. I'll call and see what I can do.

FRITZ: Kurt, you really let me down. You promised to have the stuff here today and it's not here. If I don't get delivery by tomorrow I'm going to have to close down one line. You know what the boss is going to say about that. I'm going to tell him you didn't deliver when you said you would.

Now the untangling procedure begins. Everybody's defense mechanism automatically clicks on. Long, frustrating hours will be spent at buck-passing and trying to solve what is now an emergency. If the line shuts down, the company's profits will be compromised.

Who is to blame for this oversimplified but not untypical situation?

Both men, but mostly Kurt the purchasing agent. He made a promise without clarifying what he was being asked to do, and without clarifying what he was agreeing to do.

A broken promise is expensive. It is expensive to fix or to replace or to settle. It makes everybody involved feel bad. It stains reputations. It weakens relationships. It wastes time. It makes you lose sleep.

All of this can be avoided. How? Easy.

Don't make promises you can't keep.

Don't make promises you don't fully intend to keep.

Don't make promises that are not clearly spelled out. If there are more than two or three very specific details involved, put them in writing.

Don't commit yourself with a promise where the

cost of keeping it could go up faster than the value you get in return.

Be careful about whom you authorize to make promises for you.

And then: Keep every promise you make. In fact, go further: if there is a question about what you promised, settle it by satisfying the other fellow rather than yourself. He is probably at least partly right anyway.

This doesn't mean you should be a pushover. If you are going to keep your promises, then expect other people to keep theirs to you. Force them to do so if necessary.

The time to consider your self-interest, though, is before you make a promise, not afterwards. Ask for what you want from the deal—in specifics—before you promise what you know you can deliver.

Size up the person you are dealing with. With some, a handshake, a nod, or a simple "Okay" is enough. With others, you need a lawyer to dot the i's and witness the signatures.

It is expensive as hell to keep all your promises.

It is a lot more expensive, directly and indirectly, not to keep them.

So keep them or don't make them in the first place. It's one big way to make yourself distinctive.

Never assume that others are operating under the same rules you are.

People who play by the rules are the people who make business work.

Granted, there is no shortage of thieves, liars, cheats, and connivers in business. These characters casually shift their standards of conduct to match their momentary self-interest.

Nevertheless, the great majority of people in business do try to play more or less by the rules.

The problem is that everybody's rules are different.

Football players and baseball players are lucky. They have unequivocal rules to play by. Everybody knows exactly which rules and penalties apply to each conceivable situation in the game.

People in business are not so lucky. Most of what we do is not covered by any universally accepted rules. We do have the good fortune to enjoy the services of the Internal Revenue Service, the Securities and Exchange Commission, the Interstate Commerce Commission, and dozens of other regulatory agencies. We also have the principles of management, written contracts of all sorts, the courts, and the law of supply and demand. These, however, provide rules covering only specific parts of the business game. They do not provide any standards of acceptable performance for us to follow as individuals in our day-to-day, man-to-man dealings with each other. Yet it is this interaction of individuals—working together or struggling and competing—that provides the basic building blocks with which the whole complex of business is constructed.

There are, of course, some basic rules that most people in business accept.

For example, most people pay homage to the basic rule of honesty in business. Almost everybody considers himself honest.* Yet all of us do dishonest things which we then proceed to justify to ourselves. It is not exactly

---

* The few who admit to being dishonest are, in this respect at least, probably the most honest of all.

that we break the basic rule of honesty. It is just that we bend it. How far we bend it, and in what direction, depends in part on our individual code of conduct and, probably, the circumstances. What you do I may consider dishonest. What I do you may consider reprehensible. Yet we are each following our own rules.

When you stop and think about it, you realize that it would be as impossible for others to play by your rules as it would be for you to play by everybody else's rules. You could abandon your rules and adopt the rules of one other person, but that would still leave an ocean of other people in business whose rules are all different.

Despite all the evidence to the contrary, most people in business continue to fall into the trap of carelessly assuming that others are operating under the same rules they themselves are. As a result, most business people make themselves extremely vulnerable to unpleasant surprises.

The illogical assumption goes like this: "Since I wouldn't think of doing such-and-such to so-and-so, then so-and-so won't do such-and-such to me." Then—Wham! —so-and-so not only does such-and-such to you when you least expect it, but he adds insult to injury by making clear that he feels perfectly justified in what he has done. Again: his rules versus your rules.

It is well to get rid of your illusions, but don't be disappointed by the fact that some people in business play dirty. It is simply the reality of business. There are dirty players and clean players and even the clean players may do things that are dirty according to your rules.

The way to deal with this reality is to follow these guides:

1. Mentally divide the people you work with into two groups: the majority who do play by the rules, albeit their own rules, and the minority whose only rule is immediate self-interest. Watch this second group like a hawk and be ready for anything from them.

2. For each individual in the larger group, try to determine what rules he is playing by. Don't just ask him; what he tells you may be the rules he knows he should be playing by, not the rules he is playing by. Instead, uncover his rules by observing the pattern of his actions.

3. Review what your own rules are. Make sure they are valid, constructive, and consistent. Get them clear in your mind. Better yet, on paper. Stick to your rules but change them when there is good reason to do so.

4. However, don't compromise your personal code of business conduct simply because others you work with have adopted easier, more pliable standards. The best satisfaction in business is not just winning, but winning on your own terms.

There are other big advantages to establishing a clear-cut set of business rules for yourself and letting everyone know what your rules are. One advantage is that people learn to put their trust in you. That in itself is worth plenty. But on top of that, when others get to know the rules you have set for yourself, and see you following them consistently, they often tend to adopt your rules in dealing with you, or in situations where you are involved. When you see this happening, you will have solved at least part of the problem of figuring out what rules others are playing by.

The toughest part of business, especially for a beginner, is knowing what the rules *are*.

Well, there are no rules. No ready-made rules, anyway. You are forced to make your own, and then stick to them as best you can.

But bear in mind that others are struggling with the same problem you face in balancing morality and idealism against the practical realities of day-to-day dilemmas.

Be a little forgiving if people don't measure up to your standards. Bear in mind that you are probably not measuring up to theirs.

Play the business game
for all you are worth—but not as if
your life depended on it.

Many healthy people contract business cancer. The overactivity of their business lives destroys the other aspects of their lives. The sickness can be killing and it is certainly no good for their companies.

These people waste their whole lives working.

They defeat themselves.

They take business too seriously.

They work for the wrong reasons.

They forget that a job is a means to an end, not an end in itself.

Business is the most exciting game in town. It offers richer, more numerous, and more varied stimulants and satisfactions than any other form of human endeavor. That is why business attracts the best people—the smartest and most quick-witted, the most energetic and vigorous, the most highly motivated, the most creative and imaginative, the most enthusiastic, the most purposeful, hardest working, most interesting, and most adventurous people with the broadest range of skills, interests, and talents.

The problem is that because business is so exciting, businessmen get wrapped up in it. They get so excited about business that they forget why they are in it. They find themselves working for the sake of working, or because of habit, not for the rewards their jobs should produce.

This is sad enough while a man is working, but it becomes downright tragic when he stops. How many men do you know who, after devoting their full lives to business, reluctantly retire and find that they are utterly empty and lost without their jobs to cling to? They find they have become business addicts and they can't live without their work. So they lie down and die.

Take a typical example.

A young fellow starts out in business all charged up. After a few false starts he lands in an interesting job that challenges his abilities and captures his imagination. He discovers the excitement of business. He sees the potential rewards he can get if he plays his cards right.

As he moves deeper into this job of his, it gets even more exciting. He wins some victories and new horizons open up. The immediate rewards get bigger and the potential rewards get huge. The complexity of his job increases, but that just makes it more interesting. He feels himself growing in his job, and that stimulates his self-esteem.

Then, typically, he gets a little greedy, or a little too competitive, or a little impatient, and he tries to speed up the natural process of growth by overextending his reach or taking shortcuts. Trouble, of course, follows. Problems develop. Things start going wrong.

Now he has no choice; he is forced to spend long hours dealing with the problems he himself has helped to create.

Now all of his time, energy, and thinking go into business. No time now for the family. No time for the fishing trips or the shop in the basement or museums or walks in the park. Now he lies awake nights with his mental machinery grinding away on business problems.

He still plays golf, but only with business people who talk only business. Now he eats with business people and talks business; he drinks with business people and talks business; he travels with business people and talks business. He still reads, but only business and trade publications.

In sum, he is not just married to his job; he is a prisoner of it. And it is his own damn fault.

Who needs that kind of a life?

You don't.

You can't succeed as a business dilettante, of course. You must have commitment. But don't let business flatten you into a one-dimensional character. Or a chronic worrier. Or a compulsive drudge. Or, worst of all, a habitual rut-trudger.

Don't take business too seriously. It's difficult for some people to accept this idea, especially if they have been trained differently, or if they have already let business blot out their other interests and activities.

Nevertheless, it is a proven fact: when you treat business as just one of your interests, you maintain a wider angle of perspective on your job and make yourself more valuable.

If he ever was, the company man is not the man who succeeds any more. Most companies have wised up to this fact. Some, of course, still haven't. They expect you and your family to think of The Company as some great godlike being to which you dutifully display worshipful obedience and devotion twenty-four hours a day, including Saturdays, Sundays, and holidays.

On the contrary, the day you let business become your religion, or start working strictly for the satisfaction of the work itself, that is the day you begin to cop out.

You cop out not only on yourself but on your company. Any boss who thinks he is getting a bargain from an employee who is devoted to business is wrong. For one thing, the all-business man has a shallow perspective and few if any fresh ideas. He often concentrates so hard on his work that he fails to notice the changes taking place around him. Before he realizes it, he may be left so far behind that he will never catch up.

Squeeze all the satisfaction you can out of your work, but fight hard to prevent the job itself, rather than the rewards of the job, from becoming your primary motivation.

All this is not to say that you should never devote yourself exclusively to business. Sometimes you should, or must. Capturing an opportunity may depend on it. Your growth and development may depend on it. Your survival may depend on it. When you or your company face a crisis or a business storm, don't shirk; commit yourself 100 percent to business. But don't let it become a habit.

Business is a rich experience. But so is life. Don't sacrifice your life to business. It is a poor bargain.

**Never permit a situation to continue
in your company where someone can
profit from your loss.**

It is unfair of you to tempt someone to damage you
and then expect him not to.

You do a terrible disservice to anyone you leave
dangling in that position.

You force him to make a damaging choice: either

he damages you or, in his own mind at least, he damages himself by default.

Either way, you lose.

If he succumbs to the temptation you have permitted to exist, you obviously lose. But even if he resists, you place his relationship with you under heavy strain. His reasoning may be that he is in business to serve his own interests and now here he is serving yours instead. He will probably resent this and focus his resentment on you.

Self-interest permeates and colors every other consideration in business (see Rule 14). People find ways to justify serving themselves even at the expense of harming others.

To get the problem in focus, consider these typical situations.

SITUATION: You are a talented R&D man. You join an exciting little company to perfect a new product that could be worth millions. The pay is low but you are promised big rewards if the product succeeds. You breathe life into the product and it takes off. The president gives you a heavy raise but starts hinting that they really don't need a high-priced R&D man any more.

Whose fault?

Yours. You shouldn't have accepted a vague promise subject to interpretation. At the outset you should have insisted on an agreement covering the precise terms of your reward—salary, bonus, deferred compensation, stock options, royalties, or whatever.

SITUATION: You have founded a company. You bring in a bright young R&D man to perfect a new product that could be worth millions. After a year he accepts an "impossible to turn down" offer from a large company in a related field. A year after that, the other company has captured half the market for your product.

Whose fault?

Yours. When you have a prize racehorse you don't leave the stable door wide open.

SITUATION: You are the controller of a company. Your bookkeeper has been scrupulously honest for fifteen years. No need to set up controls against theft in his case. Then you discover—too late—that what he started as small-time borrowing to solve a family problem has turned into habitual stealing.

Whose fault?

Yours. If you offer temptation on a silver platter, sooner or later some people will accept it.

SITUATION: You work in an employment agency. You knock yourself out to fill a rush order from a new company for a secretary. The company refuses to pay your fee. They say they assumed the secretary would pay it. She says she assumed the company would pay it. You lose your commission plus a secretary you could have placed with a regular client.

Whose fault?

Yours. Before swinging into action you should have checked out the company and asked them to acknowledge clearly stated terms of your service.

SITUATION: You are purchasing agent in a small plant. A supplier reports he cannot fill your order for a strategic material because of a strike. A week later your plant is crippled but your competitor is still operating. Some sleuthing reveals your supplier canceled your order to satisfy your competitor whose volume is bigger.

Whose fault?

Yours. You should have foreseen that your supplier would be under pressure in this situation. If your agreement with the supplier included a penalty clause for nondelivery, he could have withstood the pressure from his bigger customer with impunity and your plant would still be operating. Lacking the penalty clause, you should have had alternate suppliers or a reserve inventory.

SITUATION: You work in a highly specialized privately owned company. In the past ten years you have learned every aspect of the business and become the dependable right hand of the president-owner. It is understood that when he retires you will take charge. Then one evening he takes you to dinner and tells you that his son, who has been living it up in Europe all these years, has decided to come home and join the company. The owner hopes you will teach his son everything you know and help groom him for the presidency.

Whose fault?

Yours, you dope. You should have recognized the son as a threat despite his lack of qualifications. Before investing ten years in a specialized job, you should have asked for a guarantee that it was not going to turn into a dead end.

If you get caught in a situation like one of these, don't get your feelings hurt. Stand up and take it like a man. You had it coming, chum. You helped create the situation or permitted it to continue. All the other fellow did was follow a fairly predictable human course.

If you look at the situation closely, you find that even when someone gets double-crossed in business he usually helped create his own trouble by lack of foresight.

One of the most positive actions you can take in

business is to eliminate these open-end situations, or avoid letting them come into being in the first place.

Think of all the trouble God could have saved us if, instead of warning Eve not to touch the forbidden fruit, He had simply omitted that one apple tree from His horticultural layout.

Granted, you don't have quite that much control over the scheme of things in your company. However, the more position and power you do have, the more responsibility you should assume for eliminating situations where one man can profit from another's loss. Just removing the temptation makes people feel better.

Regardless of your position in your company, take steps to avoid getting stuck with a heads-you-win, tails-I-lose equation. What you do and how you do it depends on the specifics of the situation. Finding the right solution is up to you.

Often the simplest and best solution is a straight-forward written agreement. Some people feel squeamish about asking a respected business contact to commit a promise to writing. They think this implies mistrust. That isn't the point. A clearly written agreement can eliminate a whole lot of wasted time, discussion, argument, and resentment later.

You can never ignore the fact that self-interest is the motor that drives the business bus. If you set yourself in opposition to someone else's self-interest, or stand in its way, you are liable to get hit by the bus.

Equally true: if you become known as the man who can find ways to unify people by eliminating conflicting interests, you will uncork a volcano of power for your company, and for yourself.

**Never underestimate the power of
the number two man.**

Ignore the number two man at your own risk.

He has a unique position. His power is circumscribed, but because it is, he tends to make optimum use of what power he has. He may not be able to say yes, but he can almost always say no. His influence is persistent.

He can clobber you if he decides to do so. For example, if you neglect him in your dealings with the number one man, he may shoot you down in flames.

Who is the number two man? He is the assistant manager, the back-up man, the helper, the junior partner, the second in command, the boss's right-hand man. Sometimes he is a she, the secretary who has been given special prerogatives or assistant-to status.

The number two man is an orbiting planet; he draws his power from the star he circles.

It is tough being a good number two man. Often, depending on the number one man, it is the toughest job in an organization. If you make his job easier, rather than tougher, you may win a friend in court. He is the wrong man to have as an enemy but a great man to have going to bat for you.

A good man in the number two slot can do wonders for any organization. Unfortunately, many number two men never perceive this reality; they accept the limitations of the job at face value and never apply their imagination to uncover the latent power of the position. Others, of course, are not equipped to do anything about it even if they did understand the possibilities of the job.

There are all kinds of number two men. Some are frustrated number one men and they hate being overshadowed. Some are the power behind the throne; their influence is such that they actually make the number one man's decisions for him.

Then there is the jealous number two man. He resents anyone's relationship with the number one man but his own.

There are protective number two men, contented

number two men, sensitive number two men, self-appointed number two men, insecure number two men, cooperative number two men, redundant number two men, permanent number two men, and every other kind of number two man you can imagine.

Here are a couple of good things to remember in dealing with number two men regardless of what kind they are or how enlightened they are:

First, never short-circuit the number two man in your dealings with the number one man. Go through him, not over, under, or around him. Deal directly with his boss only after the number two man makes clear that you have his consent to do so. Even then, never fail to keep the number two man informed. If he objects to a decision you and his boss have made, let him decide what to do. Tell him you will hold back until he discusses it with the boss himself or gives you a green light.

If you leave the number two man out, or try to force a decision past him with a power play, it may be the last chance you get to deal with the number one man directly.

Second, when you need help, the number two man is often the best place to get it. In many organizations, because the number two man plays second fiddle, he is overlooked as a resource by other people in the organization. Yet because of his close proximity to the boss, the number two man often can, for example, counsel you on how to shape an idea to make it most acceptable to the boss. Having helped you in this way, he is then more likely to take an interest in the idea and help you sell it.

Now, if you happen to be a number one man, here are some good rules for you to follow in dealing with your number two man.

First, pick the right kind of number two man. What are you looking for—a permanent helper or a man in training who can stand in for you now and eventually take your place? If you need a permanent helper, pick someone whose strengths will cover your weaknesses and who is going to be satisfied to stay in the role of an assistant. If you want to train your number two man to take your place, pick a man with the same drive you have and skills to match your own—or perhaps the skills you know you should have for your job.

Second, take as much ambiguity out of the number two man's job as possible. It is hard enough being a number two man without the added problem of not really knowing what your job is. Yet this is the common plight of number two men, and it is almost always the number one man's fault. Tell him exactly what his job is, the specifics of his responsibility, the limitations of his authority, what his goals should be, to what degree he is accountable for results, and how you are going to measure his effectiveness.

Third, build satisfaction into his job. Number two men get unhappy because they always seem to get the dirty end of the stick. Often it is because the number one man hogs all of the status, respect, authority, privileges, praise, and recognition for himself. As a number one man, you have more than enough job satisfactions. You can afford to be charitable. Share some of yours with your number two man and see how this turns him on.

Finally, here are three important rules to follow if *you* are the number two man:

First, accept the limitations of the job philosophically. In one sense, being number two man is being almost number one man. In another sense, however, there is a world of difference between one and two. Don't resent the fact that you are the subordinate; don't fight it. Don't fight your boss. Most number twos do fight it, and lose their effectiveness as a result. Winning plaudits in a supporting role is usually a necessary step to becoming a star.

Second, recognize and use all the special advantages of the job. Consider: as number two man you are in an ideal position to learn. As aide to the number one man, your job is really as big as his is. You can see how the top man does it, help him do it, and even try your hand at it yourself, without holding the responsibility. Thus, when you get to be number one, you should be able to do it better.

Third, pick the best number one man you can find to work for. By making him look even better, you make yourself look good. And the better he is, the more you learn.

The number two man is one of the most misunderstood fellows in business. His boss misunderstands him, people trying to deal with his boss misunderstand him, and he often misunderstands himself. Because he is accustomed to being misunderstood, he will probably forgive you if you misunderstand him.

But if you underrate him, or get between him and the number one man, or in any way cause him to lose face, even in his own mind, that could be the beginning of an unpleasant story.

**Express your thanks, give lots of praise,
but don't get left holding the bag.**

The more praise you give people, the better, right?
Wrong.

To hear some so-called experts talk, you would think you just can't dish out enough praise. The more the merrier, they seem to say. They might as well advise you that since your car is a fine means of transportation, you should drive it as fast as possible regardless of the road conditions.

Praise is a powerful means of rewarding and motivating people. Like all high-powered things, however, it can be useless or dangerous if you don't know how to handle it skillfully.

You know the shibboleths and quotations about giving praise. It is more blessed to give than to receive. "Vanity of vanities; all is vanity" (Ecclesiastes). You can damn by faint praise. "Never praise a sister to a sister, in the hope of your compliments reaching the proper ears" (Kipling). Give praise in public and criticism in private. "Spare me the accolade; your praise is not worth dying for" (Martial). "You can tell the quality of every man when you see how he receives praise" (Seneca).

Sayings like these are okay as far as they go. But trying to use praise effectively in business based on these rules would be like trying to handle a machine gun with only your BB-gun experience to rely on.

For one thing, praise means different things to different people.

For some people, praise is an all-purpose home remedy that heals wounds, soothes tender feelings, and smooths rumpled feathers.

For other people, praise is like a good cup of coffee. It warms them. It stimulates them. It gives them a feeling of well-being. They could learn to live without it but that occasional coffee break, or praise break, makes working a lot more fun.

Unfortunately for some people, praise isn't quite this simple. It becomes addictive. Just as there are dope fiends, there are praise fiends.

A praise fiend is a sorry case to behold. He craves lavish doses of praise to feed the consuming fire of his ego. He will do almost anything to get praise, but it requires increasingly large doses to satisfy him. You find yourself heaping indiscriminate, undiluted portions of praise on him, or her, just to keep him, or her, from suffering the pangs of withdrawal.

The problem is that sooner or later it becomes impossible to give the praise addict the quantity and quality of praise he needs to satisfy his habit. Then the real trouble begins. Starved of praise, the praise addict begins thinking that you are not giving him what he deserves. He resents it, and resents you. He has long since convinced himself that his enlarged self-image is real. Now, because of the stature he thinks he has—a false stature you helped create by stuffing him with praise—he may take whatever actions he can to punish you for your inability to continue to satisfy him. Eventually he will defeat himself, of course, probably when he suffers that terminal malady, bursting of the ego. Until that happens, however, he is potentially dangerous, like any other kind of addict deprived of his drug.

Now, having considered the dangers of too much praise, consider its positive values and uses.

Praise puts the seasoning in a job. A good cook knows just the right amount and type of spice to add to each dish. Too little or too much may destroy the success of the meal, but most gourmets agree that too little is better.

The same goes for praise.

The value of the praise you give is determined by a combination of things. How much praise you give, the kind of praise you give, to whom you give it, how you give it—all these together determine whether your praise is valuable and effective.

For example, are you a praise-giving tightwad? If so, your statement, "You're a good man, Charlie," may be received as an accolade of the highest quality. On the other hand, if you are a praise-giving spendthrift, such a brief, simple statement, devoid of perhaps your usual sparkling superlatives, could be interpreted as an insult, especially by a praise fiend or recognition hog.

Temporarily withholding praise is sometimes as powerful as giving it, or more so. You have to be careful; some individuals become lethargic when praised, like a man who contentedly goes to sleep after a satisfying meal. A good praise-giver gives satisfying portions but always leaves 'em wanting more.

Praise serves its best purpose when it is given in combination with other rewards. If a person receives high praise together with a raise and a promotion to a more interesting job, the praise really means something. If he gets the praise with the promise of a raise and promotion, he will probably accept it as a temporary substitute. If he gets the praise as a conciliatory bribe instead of a raise and promotion, forget it.

There are two kinds of praise, honest and dishonest. Dishonest praise is mere flattery. Flattery may serve a frivolous purpose in games of love, but it has no place in business. If you give dishonest praise you discredit both yourself and the person you give it to.

It is easy to distinguish the amateurs from the pros in the art of praise giving.

An amateur tends to give praise grudgingly, or in a contrived, showy manner. His insincerity shows through his smokescreen of compliments. By showing off his praise-giving ability, he is not so much giving praise as seeking it for himself.

The pro gives praise smoothly and easily. The pro may give less praise than the promiscuous amateur, but what he gives is more meaningful because of the way he gives it. Because he is a pro, praise giving seems to come naturally.

The praise pro gives praise in many different ways.

He may give praise simply by listening carefully to what you say.

He may give praise by unself-consciously recognizing a weakness of his own and thus indirectly pointing to a strength of yours.

The pro praises you as honestly to your friends as to your face.

Praise. Recognition. Acceptance. Respect. Honors. These are the things that people work for. The man has not been born who does not respond favorably to honest praise. Even money and the other tangible rewards of business are in a sense only symbols of success, and thus a form of praise.

If you want your praise-giving ability to contribute to your own success in business, never withhold praise from someone who deserves it. To do so is the same as stealing. Give a man the amount of praise he has earned or that will motivate him to earn it.

But beware of recognition thieves. They give themselves credit for other people's accomplishments. If a praise fiend or a recognition thief takes credit for your accomplishments, you may be lucky if you are left holding the bag. Usually they try to take that too.

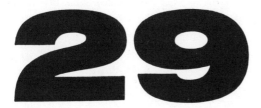

You can size up a man by the size of the problems he likes to solve.

And how he values his time.

Every organization has big-problem people and little-problem people.

You know the little-problem man. He is the fellow who fails to perceive the priorities, maybe on purpose.

In the face of critical problems, he picks out some small, easy problems that won't cause any mental strain, and devotes himself to them. He analyzes them, rearranges them, makes telephone calls about them, blows them up and stuffs them with memos. He can spend half a day thrashing around about a reference book that is missing from its shelf, or trying to decide what time to turn on the lights in the parking lot.

Meanwhile, the big-problem man has probably slayed a dragon or two.

It is a fact that more and more people in business these days are self-managing. They have discretionary jobs. *They* decide how they will use their time. They decide for themselves what they will do, how they will do it, and when. Some of these people—usually the big-problem people—milk every ounce of value out of their hours and minutes. The others waste not only their own time but the time of people around them as well. One way they do it is by playing cat and mouse with little problems.

It is also a fact that some companies spend (and waste) a fortune in time and money trying to pick winners. They use an amazing assortment of elaborate procedures, reports, scorecards, and tests.

You don't need to spend that kind of time and money to size up the people you work with. Simply give a man a chance to demonstrate the kinds of problems he likes to solve. It is a quick, simple, accurate, and cheap way to size up his brains, confidence, skill with people, experience, and talent.

Don't judge a small-problem man too harshly. Maybe the fault isn't his. Maybe he needs training, motivation, seasoning, or a different job. But be leery of the ones who refuse to budge from their routine, the single-speed plodders, the nit-pickers, schedule makers, lunch-date planners, and train catchers.

On the other hand, don't overlook the value of the small-problem man. Some people will labor arduously on routine work in order to avoid coming to grips with a real problem. Recognize this, because it is a way to get a lot of routine work done.

Just make sure the small-problem man is in a job where the problems are not too much bigger than he is. The only thing worse than a small-problem man in a big-problem job is a big-problem man in a small-problem job. That is wasteful because he will get bored to death and turn his interest elsewhere or jump ship.

Most people like to solve easy problems. It makes them feel good. A few like to tangle with tough ones. It makes them feel great. When you find a big-problem man, stick with him. He is probably a winner.

**No matter what you do, do it as if
you were competing with an equal.**

If you play tennis or any other person-to-person sport, you know how deadly dull it is to play someone half as good as you are.

You get sloppy, you lose your timing, you make mistakes you would never make against a good opponent.

Racehorses and track stars have the same problem. Even a kids' volleyball team performs best when competing against strong contenders.

It is the same in business. You cannot do your best work unless you are competing—individually, as a member of a team, or both.

The person you compete against helps determine how well you do. You need someone else to set a fast pace, or challenge you to set it.

One of the best satisfactions in business comes from sharpening your skills against someone who is at least as good as you are, even when he beats you.

Sad to say, although business attracts outstanding people, all the people in business are not outstanding. Some individuals you find yourself competing with, and some companies you find yourself competing in, are, to put it bluntly, not very sharp.

When you are working with people who are not as good as you are, the temptation is to drop down to their level of performance. This is a pivotal mistake; it sends you off in precisely the wrong direction.

It is a mistake most people make, of course, which explains why standards of performance and conduct in many companies are so depressingly, sometimes humorously lax. It also explains why most people in business throw away a good portion of their success.

When the choice presents itself, it seems so easy to take the path of least resistance. It is the direction most people are going. It is more comfortable, with fewer dangers, fewer visible threats, and fewer unknowns.

The compensation is that it also offers fewer rewards. In fact, if you look at most of the people in business, you realize that they let themselves become satisfied with pathetically unrewarding jobs. It's a tragedy. For them, business is a drag. They have to put in just about as many hours, days, and years of work as do the real performers, the business stars, but they get only a small fraction of the return on their investment.

In some companies it seems that not just the majority, but everybody is performing at a level of mediocrity. Potentially outstanding performers waste their talent; since the company doesn't expect much of them, they don't strain themselves to give much.

Granted, a company like that gets exactly what it deserves from its people. With no pacesetters, or even a coach or trainer holding a stopwatch, who cares if the competitive spirit fades away and the organization lethargically grinds its way into a rut?

If that is all the company wants, why give more?

Except for one thing. If you go along with the majority, it is not just the company that loses; you lose personally. All you are doing is getting by, instead of staying in shape and getting better as fast as it is necessary to get better if you want to be truly successful.

What do you do when the pace of the race is too slow to be challenging to you?

You have some good choices.

CHOICE ONE: Set the pace yourself; make the others match your standards. The situation creates a great opportunity for someone to step into the role of leadership— because obviously there is no leader or only a mediocre one. Since the opportunity is there, why don't you grab it? Setting a faster pace—making others come up to your standards rather than dropping down to theirs—is one of the fastest ways to call attention to yourself as a leader or potential star.

Even in a situation of pervasive lethargy, some people will usually get off their duff and give you a run for your money. If they do, you may have started something. If they don't, then go to choice two.

CHOICE TWO: Pick a new team. If you are in a position to replace people, then drop the indolent souls and let them go to an organization that is content to have sleepwalkers on the job. Replace them with people who are as good as you are, or are at least willing to try.

If you are not yet in a position to call the shots, then pick a new team by using the other option that is open to you: get out. Join a new team. Get into an organization where the caliber of competition will keep you healthy, striving, moving. One good thing about business: if you outgrow your job you can almost always find a bigger one that fits.

If you are temporarily blocked in these choices, then you still have a third choice that no one can block.

CHOICE THREE: Create your own equal, or pacesetter, to compete against. He may not exist in your company; in fact, he may not exist at all. You may have to dream him up. Most fields of business do, however, have visible champions you can use to personify a hypothetical opponent. Pick people who represent what you would like to be, or who have achieved what you would like to achieve. Then set your standards to match their standards; measure your decisions and actions against the decisions and actions you would be forced to take if you were in fact competing against these high performers.

Let's not forget the other side of the coin. Suppose you are the one who can't maintain the fast pace that has been set. Suppose you are in an organization where high performance is the standard but because of your limited experience or training you just can't keep up.

Again, you have choices. One choice is to get out—to get into a job or an organization where you can compete with people more or less on a par with you. It's like getting into the minor leagues until you are accomplished enough to play in the majors.

You wouldn't get into the ring with Joe Frazier, and you wouldn't make a fool of yourself by challenging Pancho Gonzales at tennis. In business don't take the chance of staying in a job where the best you can do is flounder.

A better choice, however, is to hang in there if you can. Even if it means clinging to your job by your teeth, you will learn more in that job than you will in any other. Consider yourself lucky that you have strong competition to learn from.

Most people in business are there for only part of the reason you are. They are content to survive, and maybe succeed a little bit.

If you have come this far in this book, it must be because your goal is to get all the success you can.

You will never get that much success unless you compete with someone who is at least your equal.

**Success has many ingredients, but
the greatest of these is confidence.**

It is so simple.

It has been said by every philosopher, every pragmatist, every victor, every champion, every star, and everyone who has been successful in business.

What they say is you can't be good at anything unless you think you are going to be good at it.

This basic law of success has been stated in a thousand different ways. It has been said so often that it sounds dumb, which is why most people in business ignore it and become losers as a result.

The law doesn't state that you will be successful if you believe you are great. It states that you can't be successful unless you believe you are great.

It usually works out like this:

If you think you are a clod, you will act like a clod, people will treat you like a clod, and you will wind up being a clod.

If you think you are pretty good, you will reflect this mediocre opinion of yourself in the way you treat yourself, people will think of you as mediocre (if they think of you at all), and you will end up a nonentity, buried somewhere in the middle.

If, on the other hand, you think you are great, or at least have enough confidence in yourself to believe you could be great, this self-image will exude through your pores, people will respond to it, you will be influenced by their response, your self-confidence will be reinforced, and you just may end up being great notwithstanding all the disqualifications you have for achieving that status.

It all comes back to a process of selling yourself. Self-confidence is only one of the ways you sell yourself to others, but it is the primary way you sell yourself to yourself. You can't convincingly sell yourself to others until you have truly sold yourself to yourself.

Most people in business do it backwards. They spend years accumulating experience, then draw their self-confidence from what they have already achieved.

What a waste of time. This is too slow. It doesn't put your self-confidence to work when you need it most.

If you want to be successful, start with self-fidence, and let your self-confidence feed itself until you have a record of accomplishment to support it.

Look at all the people you know who have become successful quickly. Isn't this the way they did it?

Keeping your self-confidence intact is not always easy. Most jobs worth having involve a steady parade of confidence-denting experiences. Setbacks. Defeats. Kicks in the face. People shooting your ideas down in flames. Ridicule. Being proved wrong after you serenely took some action you knew would work.

There is one excellent way to maintain your equilibrium in the face of these experiences. It is to hold firmly in mind that you are making your best progress when you seem to be making your least.

This may seem like double-think, but it works. It has been proved by experience over and over again. The reason it works is that it is not double-think at all. The solid fact is that even when your career seems to be in a shambles, you may in fact only be at a point of transition, moving from something good to something better.

Experienced businessmen know that they are often making their best progress when they seem to be making their least.

There is one key to maintaining confidence in your own success before it happens: believe strongly in what you are doing. If you don't believe in what you are doing, then stop doing it and start doing what you believe in.

For some people in business, the problem is not too little confidence; it is too much. Overconfidence is worse than underconfidence. It causes you to take ill-conceived gambles that usually result sooner or later in permanent damage. Underconfidence is a success inhibitor, but overconfidence is a career killer.

Here is the progression you have to watch out for: confidence breeds success, success breeds overconfidence, overconfidence breeds arrogance, and an arrogant businessman is doomed. Regardless of how much money he amasses.

Arrogance is a problem to worry about later, after you have become highly successful. In the meantime, keep your self-confidence pumped up.

Confidence, of course, comes easier when you have some experience under your belt. Especially successful experience. The more victories you have behind you, the easier it is to believe in yourself.

The nature of business is such, however, that even winners experience periods when their self-esteem is tested by a shattering series of seemingly endless defeats. For example, it is pretty darn tough to maintain your self-confidence when you have been passed over for promotion or—to make the picture worse—kicked out of your job. The only thing you can do to keep your confidence from sagging in such a situation is to work at it, and keep in mind that thousands of people in business have survived and succeeded after experiencing the same kind of setbacks that may be plaguing you.

Imagine two guys of absolutely equal measurements. They look the same, their experience is the same, their talents are the same, their goals are the same—they are perfectly matched.

Now give one of these identical twins just 10 percent

more confidence than the other, and see what happens.

You already know. Within a month the fellow with the extra self-confidence will have edged perhaps imperceptibly ahead of his counterpart. Within a year he will have widened the gap to a noticeable difference. Within ten years there will be no comparison between the success levels of the two men. The buoyancy caused by that extra measure of self-confidence will have moved one man far ahead of the other.

A man who thinks he is great usually becomes successful.

A man who knows he is great almost always does.

**Don't win too soon. You'll miss half
the fun of playing the business game.**

Business is nothing but an endless dull struggle for most people.

These are the ones who think of their jobs as work.

They get little real satisfaction out of it. Some make a lot of money, but after awhile money-making alone can become as tasteless as a diet of nothing but filet mignon.

If you want to taste all the rich satisfactions a job in business has to offer, there is a way to do it. Just make one simple mental adjustment. Stop thinking of your job as work and start thinking of it as sport—a healthy, disciplined way to perfect your style and exercise your creative talents.

Okay, maybe you have been working today—instead of playing golf or taking a hike—because you need the money. In this you may have no immediate choice. But you do have plenty of other choices. Any number of people shift occupations these days, getting out of jobs they don't enjoy and into activities they do enjoy, even though the financial rewards may be smaller in the beginning.

Instead of sitting in an office, for example, you could become a plumber, and perhaps make more money than you make now. The reason you don't is that you obviously like your job in business better than plumbing.

For the sake of argument, however, let's assume you are locked into your job for economic or other reasons. That is still no excuse for thinking of your work as *work*, rather than sport.

Work is something you do for money, or because it has to get done. A game or sport is an activity you participate in for its inherent satisfactions.

As proof that the two can be the same, consider this definition of the word *game;* see if you don't agree that it makes a pretty good definition of business too:

> *game:* a physical or mental competition played according to rules in which the participants are in direct op-

position to each other. Each side strives to win and
to prevent the other side from doing so.

Here's what you lose when you treat business, or
your own job, as work rather than sport:

1. *You lose your health.* Look at all the sick, quiv-
ering, ulcerated, hypertensioned, exhausted executives
and other "successes" you see around in business, waiting
for their heart attacks. Do you really want that kind of
success for yourself?

2. *You lose a lot of sleep.* When you think of business as work, even small problems keep you tossing and
turning at night. And when you have big problems, there
is no sense even getting into bed.

3. *You lose your job effectiveness.* The man who
thinks of his job as work usually gets into a rut. He
doesn't use his imagination, so it atrophies. He handles
his job in a mechanical way. From day to day you can
almost see his eyes getting glassier.

4. *You lose your chance to rise to the top.* Or at
least you seriously diminish your chances. Look at most
companies: Is it the pinch-faced drudges who become
the leaders, or the spirited men who obviously enjoy what
they are doing?

Now consider what you stand to gain when you treat
business, or your own job, as sport rather than work:

1. *You gain a great deal of pleasure.* You begin to
draw all the satisfaction out of your job itself, out of
the services you perform. Kids don't play baseball just
because it is fun to win. They play because it is fun to
play. The same thing applies to your job if you think of
it in the right way.

2. *You gain freedom.* That's right—freedom from

the minor annoyances of business, the things that drive
people to drink, to doctors, or just up the wall.

When you are freed from these insidious torments
and destructive tensions, you find you have renewed energies to direct into areas of business creativity.

3. *You gain satisfaction, not frustration, from the
rivalries and competition of business.* It is the quality of
the opposition that makes most games and sports enjoyable. If you think of business as a sport—a game you
are in because you want to be, a game you are going to
play seriously and as well as you can—then your competitors and rivals become the force that makes the game
worth playing, rather than crosses to bear or problems to
overcome.

4. *You gain a valuable reputation.* Treat business
like a sport and other business people will think of you
as someone who enjoys business and therefore is fun to
be with. You will become the man they want on their
team, the man who will be repeatedly moved into more
important positions because of the vigor you display in
your job. Contacts are vital in business; you will develop
more contacts if you are enjoying yourself, because people like to be with individuals who are enjoying themselves.

The biggest advantage of all is that you will not
only be thought of as successful; you will in fact become
more successful sooner. So much so, in fact, that you
will be tempted to cash in your chips and quit while you
are ahead.

The fact is that if you play the business game well,
before very many years you won't have to play it at all.

Many people in our business society these days

could support themselves comfortably without working very much. Some people do drop out, and a few are actually glad they did. The majority of those who try it, however, wish they hadn't. They discover that they enjoyed playing the business game, even though they didn't realize it at the time.

Many people dream about and talk about getting out of the business rat race. If business has become a rat race for you, it is probably because of mistakes you have made or because you are not playing the game the way it ought to be played.

If that is the case, don't resign yourself to an unsatisfying business life. And certainly don't drop out for that reason. It will label you a failure.

Instead, fix what is wrong. Change your attitude toward business. Stop putting in time. Stop just working. Start treating business as a sport.

If you are in the wrong job, get into the right one.

If you hate city life, move to one of the increasing numbers of companies that are located in pastoral country settings.

If you don't like the reckless way people around you are playing the game, keep your guard up but play by your own rules, or get into a company where they play more to your liking.

If your job is dreary, get into a company where people play with the kind of spirit and degree of competitiveness you like. Get out of the turtle race and into a horse race.

You can make your business career into anything you want it to be. It is all there in business—all the satisfactions to be gotten out of life.

You want to devote your life to serving mankind? Fine. Do it in business.

You want to become rich and famous? Fine. Do it in business.

You want freedom to live your life in your own style? Fine. Business can give you that too.

Whatever it is you want out of your life—travel, security, variety, love, leisure, wealth, creative expression, excitement—you can get more of it as a success in business than in any other way.

So why win too soon? Set your goals high enough in the first place, and keep moving them higher, so you can stretch the enjoyment of business throughout your career. When it comes time for retirement, have at least one new business career ready to step into.

You have to spend your life doing something. Why not spend it doing something constructive, rewarding, and—if you do it right—thoroughly satisfying?

Each of us measures success differently. But we can all agree that success means being creatively productive in a highly rewarding way.

Henry David Thoreau said, "Are you one of the ninety-seven who fail, or the three who succeed? Answer me . . . and then perhaps I may look at your baubles and find them ornamental. The cart before the horse is neither beautiful nor useful."

author's money-back guarantee

This book is guaranteed to make you measurably more successful than you are.

If you apply the rules and are not fully satisfied, keep the book and return the dust jacket to me care of AMA in New York. Include a letter explaining how you applied the rules and why they don't work. If you are honestly convinced these ground rules can't help you, I will gladly refund my royalty on your copy.

Like all guarantees, this one is limited by certain conditional clauses, to wit:

1. *The warranty is invalidated if you follow some of the rules but fail to follow all of them.* No game can be played using some rules and violating others.

Some of the rules may seem to contradict each other. For example, Rule 13 cautions you to make as few mistakes as possible; Rule 22 shows you that you cannot be successful without making mistakes. Both rules are valid. Each must be tempered by the other. It is up to you to keep all the rules in balance.

2. *The warranty is invalidated if you fail to adjust the rules to fit the conditions under which you work.* This is not a "how to" book. It is a "what to" book. It gives you the material you need to build a solid code of personal business practice. You must adapt the rules to your own style. Use the rules as flexible guides, not dogma.

3. *The warranty is invalidated if you fail to break the rules occasionally.* These rules like all rules must at times be broken. All the more reason to learn them. If you break these rules carelessly or ignorantly, you will probably diminish your success, or destroy your chances completely. But if you understand and respect the rules, and occasionally break them thoughtfully and with full awareness of what you are doing, your success may be helped. Business is practical, not ideal. Be realistic.

4. *This warranty is invalidated if you fail to apply the rules with a strong, unswerving desire to be successful on your own terms.* These rules cannot take the place of motivation, talent, knowledge, personality, or a willingness to continue to grow and learn regardless of your age or past successes. What the rules can do is to multiply the power of these forces that are indispensable to success.